Snowball Quilt Simplified

Patricia Knoechel

Thank you Mother Earth
Since the earliest times,
Man has been inspired by nature
to create art.
The symbols we use in our quilts:
The snowballs,
The snowflakes,
The stars and flowers
Have been inspired
through the beauty
and gifts
of nature.
We show our appreciation
by giving thanks,
sharing with others
and recycling.
Let's celebrate our planet every day!

My sincere gratitude to these special people:

To *Jean Weller*, for her Basic Snowball quilt on the inside back cover.

To *Cora Eaton*, for location photos in her cabin in Idyllwild, California.

To *Deborah O' Brien*, for helpful hints in making the Snowball.

To *Harriet Hargrave*, for designing the Snowflake stencil.

To *Eleanor Burns*, my sister and my hero.

Published by Quilt in a Day, Inc.

1955 Diamond Street, San Marcos, CA 92069

Copyright © 1993 by Patricia Knoechel

ISBN - 0-922705-41-0

Editor Eleanor Burns

Art Direction Merritt Voigtlander

Desktop Publishing Susan Sells

Photography Wayne Norton

            David Steutel

Table of Contents

Introduction

As I remember from my childhood in Pennsylvania, a snowball could become a snowman, or a snow fort, or even bring tears to the eyes of a wounded playmate. Now that I'm a quilter, I've discovered that making snowballs is a form of play that does not require warm mittens and snowboots. And one doesn't have to wait for the cold winter months for the fun to begin.

As I bounced the snowball around, I discovered that it can take on a new look, depending on the shapes and values surrounding it. Combined with a colorful nine-patch, the snowball offers an endless variety of possibilities and projects.

The Basic Snowball Quilt (page 10) is an easy beginner project, with all of the snowballs and nine-patch blocks being identical. If you want a unique look, the Scrap Snowball Quilt is a variation using the basic snowball technique. A more challenging quilt is the Star Snowball Quilt (page 41) with three different nine-patch blocks.

Are you one of those quilters (like me) who loves to make quilt tops, but can never find time to finish? The Stained Glass Swag is designed just for you (and me). With the quilt top draped over a curtain rod, the sunlight shines through the swag. The darkened seam allowances give a stained glass effect.

The simplicity of the snowball block allows numerous possibilities for embellishment. You may choose to leave it plain or make it fancy with the addition of doilies or snowflake quilting. As a friendship quilt, the snowball block has wide open spaces for signing names and personal messages.

The "Memories" Wallhanging that I made for my parents' fifty-first anniversary was a most rewarding and endearing experience. Through the photo transfer process, I watched my childhood memories come to life on fabric. And then my creativity soared as I combined fabric cutouts and other embellishments. Moments become memories. Share those special moments in time with your loved ones through a Memory Quilt.

On those cold winter days
Stay inside and play.
You don't have to go out into the snow
To make snowballs.

So now is the time.
Get out your favorite playthings:
Your sewing machine, your tools,
Your favorite colors.

You'll be snowballed with possibilities!

Supplies

100% cotton fabric, 44" wide (No directional fabrics)

Sewing machine with ¼" presser foot

All purpose neutral thread

Large rotary cutter with sharp blade

Gridded cutting mat 18" x 24"

Plexiglass rulers:
　　6" x 6"
　　6" x 24"
　　6" x 12"

12½" Square Up

Extra long quilter's pins

Pencil

Scissors

Ironing board

Steam iron

Machine quilting finish:
　　Walking foot
　　1" Safety pins and "Kwik Klip" tool
　　Fine nylon invisible thread or neutral to match
　　Snowball or Star Chain
　　Snowflake stencil for free-motion quilting
　　Fabric marker such as silver pencil or chalk
　　liner to mark stencil lines
　　Cloth eraser for removing stencil lines
　　Masking tape or 2" binder clips
　　Thin batting

Optional Doilies
　　4" to 5" Round doilies, crocheted or
　　Battenburg, one for each Snowball

"Memories" Wallhanging
　　Follow specific supplies listed on page 88.

Planning Your Quilt

You may select any of three general "looks." The easiest is the **Basic Snowball** which has all identical **Nine-Patch blocks** and **Snowball blocks**.

The **Scrap Snowball**, a more random look, uses the same assembly technique described with the **Basic Snowball**.

Basic Snowball

In the **Nine-Patch**, repeat the light **Snowball** fabric at the center, and use four different medium to dark fabrics. Position these four fabrics twice, in opposite sides or corners.

Use another medium or dark fabric for all **Snowball corners**.

Start with Fabric Selection on page 10.

Basic Scrap Quilt

Use a random arrangement of scrap fabrics for the **Nine-Patch**.

Use a light for the **Snowball**. The **Snowball** corners can be in matching fabrics or as an assortment.

Start Basic Scrap Quilt on page 12.

Or you may select the **Star Snowball** which includes three different **Nine-Patch blocks** and one **Snowball block**.

Star Snowball

The **Snowball Blocks** are identical, with two fabrics used on the corners of opposite sides.

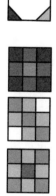

There are **three different Nine-Patch blocks:**

The **Star Block** forms the main body of the star.

The **Chain Blocks** form a connecting chain running diagonally in opposite directions.

At the **Chain Link**, the diagonal chains intersect.

Start with Fabric Selection on page 41.

Star Scrap Quilt

Make each **Star** a different color, or choose two alternating **Star** colors. Use consistent fabrics throughout the **Chain Blocks** and **Chain Links.** Start Star Scrap Quilt on page 43.

Cutting Techniques

Cutting 2 ¾" Strips

Use a rotary cutter and 6" x 24" ruler on a gridded cutting mat. Reverse this procedure if you are left handed.

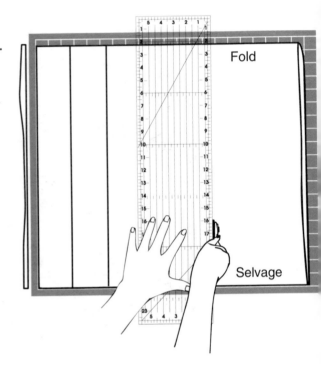

1. Make a nick on the edge and tear fabric from selvage to selvage to put the fabric on the straight-of-the-grain.

2. Fold the fabric in half, matching the torn straight edge.

3. With the fold of the fabric at the top, line up the torn edge of fabric on the gridded cutting mat with the left edge extended slightly to the left of zero.

4. Line up the right edge of ruler on zero.

5. Spread the fingers of your left hand to hold the ruler firmly. With rotary cutter in your right hand, begin cutting with the blade against the edge of the ruler. Firmly cut away from you, trimming the torn edge.

6. Lift and position the ruler with 2 ¾" ruler lines on the just cut edge. Use the top of ruler as a "T" square. Cut the number of strips of each fabric according to your yardage chart.

7. Check strips periodically for straightness. If strip becomes "V" shaped when opened, you need to restraighten the edge.

8. **Stack strips and label according to fabric number.**

Cutting Strips in Half

Depending on your size quilt, only one half of a strip may be needed. Cut on the center crease of the strip, making two 22" x 2 ¾" strips.

Cutting 2 ¾" Squares for Snowball Corners

1. Carefully line up and stack two folded strips with fold on right.

2. Use the 6" x 6" ruler to square off the selvage edges on the left.

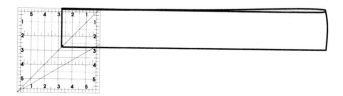

3. Measure in and cut every 2 ¾" using the ruler lines as a guide. At the fold, unfold and cut one more square, for a total of 15 squares from each strip.

The Snowball squares will be cut later, based on the size of your Nine-Patch blocks.

Fabric Selection for the Basic Snowball

First select a multi-colored fabric which contains two main color families. It may be used in either the Nine-Patch or in the Snowball Corners. Repeat the multi-colored print in the wide border.

Refer to "fussy cut" found on page 13.

Nine-Patch Block

Select four fabrics **1, 2, 3, and 4,** of similar value such as all mediums. If an old-fashioned look is preferred, select light medium fabrics. Select a variety of colors or print scales. Each fabric is used twice in the Nine-Patch. Position each fabric on two opposite sides or two opposite corners.

A light fabric **5** is placed in the center of the Nine-Patch and repeats in the Snowball.

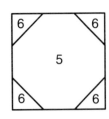

Snowball Block

For the Snowball octagon, select a light fabric, **5,** such as a muslin or a printed muslin. *As a variation, you may choose a dark Snowball with light to medium values in the Nine-Patch and Snowball Corners.*

For the Snowball Corners select another medium fabric, **6,** in a small print or one that appears solid from a distance.

The Scrap Quilt and some fabric variations are shown on pages 12 and 13.

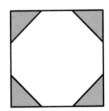

Basic Snowball Paste Up Sheet

Cut out 1¼" squares and paste according to fabric number:

1	2	3	4	5	6

Nine-Patch

1	4	3
2	5	2
3	4	1

Snowball

6		6
	5	
6		6

Scrap Quilt

The Scrap Quilt follows the Basic Snowball instructions, using random strips instead of the designated fabrics 1, 2, 3 and 4.

1. Limit your fabric selection to two or three colors, or choose colors randomly.

Nine-Patch Fabrics: From an assortment of medium or dark fabrics, cut selvage to selvage strips.

Cut 2 ¾" scrap strips:

Baby	9
Lap	18
Twin	27
Double/Queen	36
King	45

Snowball Fabric: Select a light fabric such as a muslin or a printed muslin.

Baby	⅔ yd
Lap	1 ⅛ yds
Twin	1 ½ yds
Double/Queen	2 ¼ yds
King	2 ⅔ yds

2. For remaining yardage, find your quilt size in the Basic Snowball Yardage Charts on pages 14 through 18. Start with Snowball Corners.

   Snowball Corners: All matching corners: Purchase and cut squares according to your size quilt.

   Or Random Scrap Corners: Cut 2 ¾" squares according to your size quilt.

3. Follow the Basic Snowball Nine-Patch assembly instructions starting on page 19. When making Sections A, B and C, disregard the fabric selections. Choose strips randomly to make the number of sections required for your size quilt.

Baby	1 each: ABC
Lap	2 each: ABC
Twin	3 each: ABC
Double/Queen	4 each: ABC
King	5 each: ABC

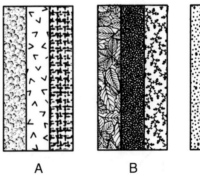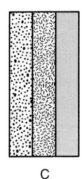

A   B   C

4. Before sewing the three-piece sections together, (on page 25) shuffle the pieces to create random looking blocks. Because of seam pressing, Section B should be separate from Sections A and C.

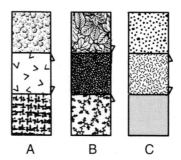

A   B   C

5. When sewing corner squares onto Snowball blocks, (on page 34) randomize squares before assembly-line sewing. (Maintain consistency in drawn lines.)

Fabric Variations

1. For the center square of the Nine-Patch, make a "fussy cut" from a floral print. Cut a 2 ¾" square of template plastic. Outline flower on template to reposition and cut identical squares. When making Section B on page 21, sew squares in place of center strip.

   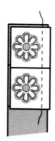   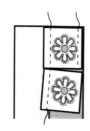

2. For a "fussy cut" in the Snowball block, select fabric with large isolated flowers, each fitting within a 7" square. Do not make template or cut fabric until Nine-Patch is completed.

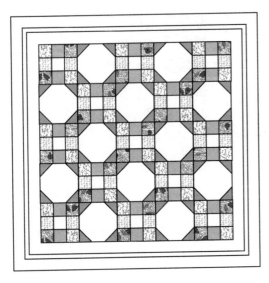

Yardage and Cutting Charts

Basic Baby Quilt

25 Blocks: 5 across x 5 down
Approximate Finished Size 42" x 42"

13 Nine-Patches
12 Snowballs

Fabrics 1, 2, 3, 4				
Medium to Dark	¼ yd each	Nine-Patch		Cut (2) strips from each fabric, 2 ¾" x 44"
Fabric 5				
Light, at least 44" wide	¾ yd	Nine-Patch		Cut (1) strip, 2 ¾" x 44"
		Snowball		Cut (12) squares later
		Second Border (optional)		Cut (4) strips, 1 ¼" x 44"
Fabric 6				
Medium	½ yd	Snowball Corners		Cut (4) strips, 2 ¾" x 44" into (48) 2 ¾" squares
First Border				
Medium to Dark	⅓ yd			Cut (4) strips, 2" x 44"
Third Border				
Medium	½ yd			Cut (4) strips, 3" x 44"
Binding				
	½ yd			Cut (4) strips, 3" x 44"
Backing				
	1 ⅜ yds			
Batting				
	46" x 46"			

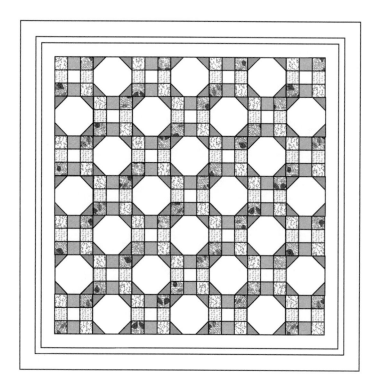

Basic Lap Quilt

49 Blocks: 7 across x 7 down
Approximate Finished Size 58" x 58"

25 Nine-Patches
24 Snowballs

Fabrics 1, 2, 3, 4				
Medium to Dark	½ yd each	Nine-Patch		Cut (4) strips from each fabric, 2 ¾" x 44"
Fabric 5				
Light, at least 44" wide	1 ¼ yds	Nine-Patch		Cut (2) strips, 2 ¾" x 44"
		Snowball		Cut (24) squares later
		Second Border (optional)		Cut (5) strips, 1 ½" x 44"
Fabric 6				
Medium	⅔ yd	Snowball Corners		Cut (7) strips, 2 ¾" x 44" into (96) 2 ¾" squares
First Border				
Medium to Dark	⅜ yd			Cut (5) strips, 2" x 44"
Third Border				
Medium	1 yd			Cut (6) strips, 4 ½" x 44"
Binding				
	⅝ yd			Cut (6) strips, 3" x 44"
Backing				
	3 ¾ yds			Cut (2) equal pieces
Batting				
	62" x 62"			

Basic Twin Quilt

84 Blocks: 7 across x 12 down
Approximate Finished Size 66" x 98"

42 Nine-Patches
42 Snowballs

Fabrics 1, 2, 3, 4				
Medium to Dark	⅝ yd each	Nine-Patch		Cut (6) strips from each fabric, 2 ¾" x 44"
Fabric 5				
Light, at least 44" wide	1 ⅞ yds	Nine-Patch Snowball		Cut (3) strips, 2 ¾" x 44" Cut (42) squares later
Fabric 6				
Medium	1 ¼ yds	Snowball Corners		Cut (12) strips, 2 ¾" x 44" into (168) 2 ¾" squares
First Border				
Medium to Dark	1 yd			Cut (7) strips, 4" x 44"
Second Border				
Light	½ yd			Cut (7) strips, 2" x 44"
Third Border				
Medium	1 ½ yds			Cut (8) strips, 6" x 44"
Binding				
	⅞ yd			Cut (8) strips, 3" x 44"
Backing				
	6 yds			Cut (2) equal pieces
Batting				
	70" x 102"			

Basic Double and Queen Quilts

117 Blocks: 9 across x 13 down
Approximate Finished Size 80" x 104"
Add wider borders to Queen 86" x 110"

59 Nine-Patches
58 Snowballs

Fabrics 1, 2, 3, 4			
Medium to Dark	¾ yd each	Nine-Patch	Cut (8) strips from each fabric, 2 ¾" x 44"
Fabric 5			
Light, at least 44" wide	2 ⅝ yds	Nine-Patch Snowball	Cut (4) strips, 2 ¾" x 44" Cut (58) squares later
Fabric 6			
Medium	1 ½ yds	Snowball Corners	Cut (16) strips, 2 ¾" x 44" into (232) 2 ¾" squares
First Border			
Medium to Dark Double	1 yd		Cut (8) strips, 3 ½" x 44"
Queen	1 ⅛ yds		Cut (8) strips, 4 ½" x 44"
Second Border			
Light Double	1 ¼ yds		Cut (8) strips, 4 ½" x 44"
Queen	1 ⅜ yds		Cut (8) strips, 5 ½" x 44"
Third Border			
Medium Double	1 ⅞ yds		Cut (9) strips, 6 ½" x 44"
Queen	2 ¼ yds		Cut (9) strips, 7 ½" x 44"
Binding			
Double	1 yd		Cut (9) strips, 3" x 44"
Queen	1 yd		Cut (10) strips, 3" x 44"
Backing			
Double	7 yds		Cut (2) equal pieces
Queen	8 ½ yds		Cut (3) equal pieces
Batting			
Double	86" x 110"		
Queen	94" x 116"		

Basic King Quilt

143 Blocks: 11 across x 13 down
Approximate Finished Size 96" x 108"

72 Nine-Patches
71 Snowballs

Fabrics 1, 2, 3, 4			
Medium to Dark	1 yd each	Nine-Patch	Cut (10) strips from each fabric, 2 ¾" x 44"
Fabric 5			
Light, at least 44" wide	3 ½ yds	Nine-Patch Snowball	Cut (5) strips, 2 ¾" x 44" Cut (71) squares later
Fabric 6			
Medium	1 ¾ yds	Snowball Corners	Cut (19) strips, 2 ¾" x 44" into (284) 2 ¾" squares
First Border			
Medium to Dark	1 yd		Cut (8) strips, 3 ½" x 44"
Second Border			
Light	1 ½ yds		Cut (9) strips, 5 ½" x 44"
Third Border			
Medium	2 ¼ yds		Cut (10) strips, 7" x 44"
Binding			
	1 yd		Cut (10) strips, 3" x 44"
Backing			
	9 yds		Cut (3) equal pieces
Batting			
	102" x 114"		

Basic Snowball Quilt

 Making the Nine-Patch

Make this many blocks:

Baby	13
Lap	25
Twin	42
Double/Queen	59
King	72

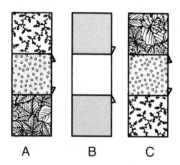

A   B   C

The completed block is made of Sections A, B and C. Sections A and C are identical and are made at the same time. Section C is turned around when the sections are sewn together.

Making Sections A and C

1. Count out this many 2 ¾" strips:

	Fabric 1	*Fabric 2*	*Fabric 3*
Baby	2	2	2
Lap	4	4	4
Twin	6	6	6
Double/Queen	8	8	8
King	10	10	10

2. Arrange your strips in this order:

3. Sizes larger than Baby, stack strips.

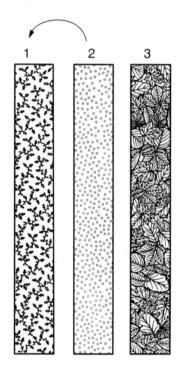

1   2   3

4. Flip a strip **2** onto a **1**, right sides together.

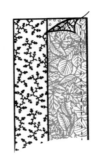

5. Set your machine to 15 stitches per inch, or 2 to 2.5 on machines with stitch selections from 1 to 4.

6. Sew a few inches with an accurate ¼" seam allowance. Stop sewing and measure the seam. Make an adjustment if necessary. An accurate, consistent seam allowance is critical to the assembly of the block. Seams will match better and your unfinished block will square up to 7".

7. Assembly-line sew the strips together by butting one pair after the other. Do not raise presser foot or clip threads. Assembly-line sew all strips from the first two stacks.

8. Open strips and flip the **3** onto **2**, and sew right sides together as before.

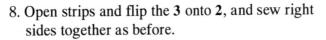

9. Clip connecting threads.

10. Divide the sections equally in half and label them Section A and Section C. Set aside. You will have this many in each Section stack:

Baby	1
Lap	2
Twin	3
Double/Queen	4
King	5

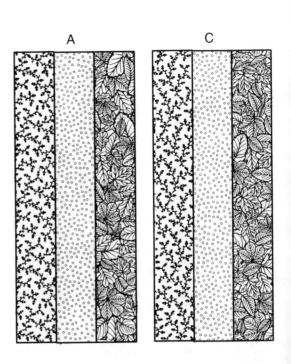

A   C

▢▢▢ Making Section B

Section B makes the center of the Nine-Patch. If you have selected a "fussy cut" for the center square, use in place of Fabric 5.

1. Count out this many 2 ¾" strips:

	Fabric 4	Fabric 5
Baby	2	1
Lap	4	2
Twin	6	3
Double/Queen	8	4
King	10	5

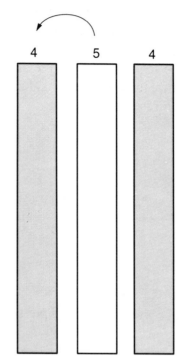

2. Divide the **4** strips equally in half.

3. Arrange your strips in this order:
   Sizes larger than Baby, stack strips.

4. Flip a strip **5** onto a **4**, and sew right sides together.

5. For sizes larger than Baby, assembly-line sew all strips.

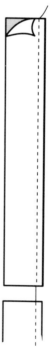

6. Open strips and assembly-line sew the remaining **4** onto **5**.

7. Clip connecting threads and label Section B.

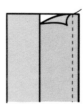

Pressing the Sections

Press seams of Section B away from the center.

Place section right side up on ironing board with center strip curled over front edge of board. Using a gentle sweeping motion, press top strip up. Be careful not to press folds into the seam line. After pressing length of top strip, turn section around and press remaining strip in same manner.

The wrong side, when pressed, will look like this.

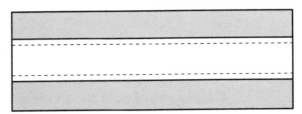

Section B

Press seams of Sections A and C toward the center.

Place section wrong side up on ironing board. Press seams toward center strip. Turn section right side up and press again. Press out any folds in seam line.

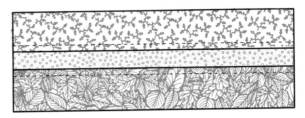

Sections A and C

Cutting Sections A and B

1. Place Section A right side up on the cutting mat with **Fabric 1 across the top edge.** For sizes larger than Baby, always position Section A with Fabric **1** across the top.

2. Place Section B right sides together onto Section A. Carefully line up the top and left edges. Run your hand along the seams to interlock them.

3. With a 6"x12" ruler and rotary cutter, square off the left edge to straighten and remove the selvage.

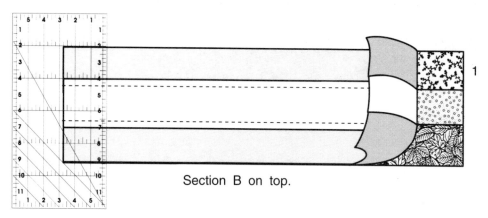

Section B on top.

4. Use the ruler lines to measure in 2 ¾", and cut the paired pieces.

5. For accurate cutting, line up one of the horizontal ruler lines with a fabric strip below. This will prevent your cuts from running off angle. Make straightening cuts if you lose that right angle.

6. Layer cut every 2 ¾", carefully lifting, moving, and lining up the ruler. You should cut 15 pairs from each layered section.

7. As you cut each pair, carefully place it onto a large plexiglass ruler for convenience in carrying the pieces to the sewing machine.

Cut this many pairs:

Baby	13
Lap	25
Twin	42
Double/Queen	59
King	72

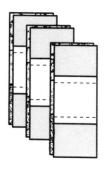

Note: Most sewers will get 15 cuts across. If you have short strips or cutting errors, you may need to assemble more shorter sections to get your required number. Allowance has been given in the yardage charts.

8. Set aside these A/B pairs

Cutting Section C

1. Place Section C right side up on the cutting mat with **Fabric 3 along top edge**. Square off the left edge to straighten and remove the selvage. Cut the pieces every 2 ¾". Cut through single thickness only.

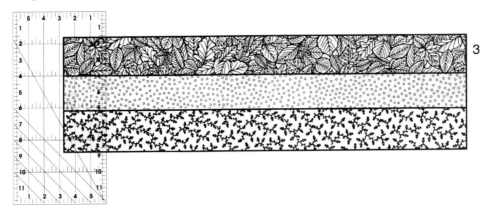

2. Cut and stack the same number of pieces as paired A/B's.

Cut this many pieces:

Baby	13
Lap	25
Twin	42
Double/Queen	59
King	72

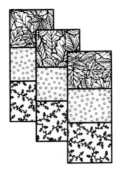

Sewing the Sections Together

Sections A and B:

1. Flip open one of the paired pieces to check for proper arrangement of strips. Turn to correct if necessary. Fabric **1** is at the top of A.

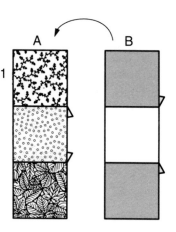

2. Pick up a paired piece A/B and line up the first seams interlocking with one seam up and the other seam down.

   Fingerpinning:
   Hold your finger over the seam as you approach it. Once sewn, line up the second seams, stretching to meet if necessary. Again place your finger over the second seam as it is approached.

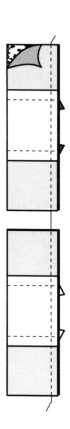

3. Assembly-line sew by butting one pair after the other. Sew all paired A/B in the stack. Do not clip connecting threads.

Adding Section C

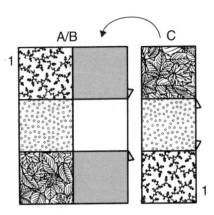

1. Beginning with the first A/B pair, open and position next to a Section C piece. Check for proper arrangement. **Be certain that matching fabrics will be in opposite corners of the Nine-Patch.**

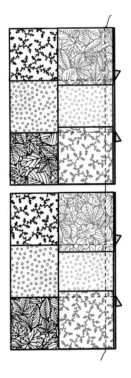

2. Flip C right sides together onto the A/B.

3. Finger pin to match seams as you assembly-line sew all pieces from the stack.

4. Clip the connecting threads.

5. Press the seams away from center.

   Press from both the right and wrong sides to press out any folds in the seams.

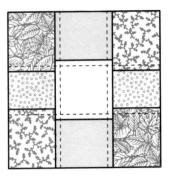

Squaring Nine-Patches

Squaring the blocks to the same size is time consuming, but results in an easily assembled quilt.

1. Using a Square Up ruler, measure several blocks to find an average size.

   In most cases, the blocks will square up to 7".

2. If your blocks measure slightly ($1/8$") over 7" square, square them to 7". Your blocks may all square to 7 $1/8$" or 6 $7/8$" depending on your seam allowance. **(Do not trim off more than $1/8$" from any one side.)** Over trimming may create problems later when matching seams.

3. First Trim: Position the diagonal line of the ruler to cross the matched center seams. Center your squaring size measurement, for example 7". Look at all four sides in order to trim equally.

   Sliver trim the right and top edges of the block.

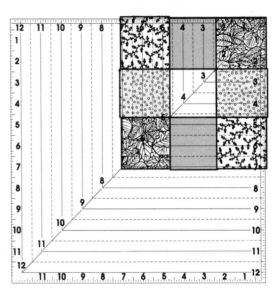

4. Second Trim: Turn the block around with the two trimmed edges lining up on your squaring size, for example 7".

   Sliver trim the two remaining edges of the block.

5. If one edge of a block "dips in" considerably less than your squaring size, mark it with a pin. An adjustment can be made later in the seam allowance.

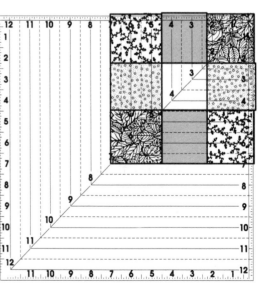

6. Record the size of your squared Nine-Patches:_____

Basic Snowball Blocks

Cutting the Light Strips

The fabric should measure at least 44" from selvage to selvage in order to get 6 generous 7" squares across a width. Yardage allows one extra strip for cutting errors.

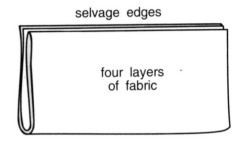

selvage edges

four layers
of fabric

1. Place your light snowball fabric on the cutting mat with the fold at the bottom. Line up the two selvage edges along the entire length of the fabric.

2. Bring the folded edge up to line up with the selvage edges. Carefully line up the entire length of the fabric to avoid crooked strips.

3. Place the Square Up ruler along the left edge of the fabric. Line up the top edge of the ruler with the selvage/fold. Square off the left edge of the fabric, being careful to cut through all four thicknesses.

By working on the left corner of a table, you can square off by moving to the left side of the table. Stand in front of the table while cutting strips.

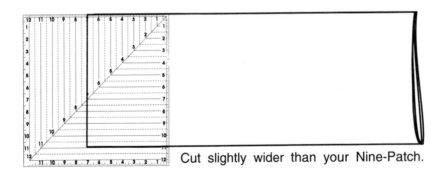

Cut slightly wider than your Nine-Patch.

4. Because the Snowball Block "shrinks" slightly after the corners are sewn, the **light strips** are **cut slightly wider than your Nine-Patch measurement**. Look at the inch lines on your quilting ruler. **Add the width of the ruler line to the size of your Nine-Patch.**

Cut this many strips:

Baby	2
Lap	4
Twin	7
Double/Queen	10
King	12

As you cut your strips, unfold and check periodically for straightness. Straighten the left edge when necessary.

Cutting the Snowball Squares:

1. With the square ruler, square off the left edge of the folded strip to straighten and remove the selvages. Check left edge to be certain you are cutting through two layers.

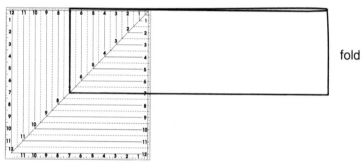

fold

Cut slightly wider than your Nine-Patch.

2. Use the ruler lines to measure in your strip width (for example, 7" plus the width of the ruler line). For all sizes larger than wallhanging: **Cut six squares per strip.**

Cut this many squares:

Baby	12
Lap	24
Twin	42
Double/Queen	58
King	71

Marking the Snowball Corners

1. Count out this many 2 ¾" squares of Fabric **6**:

Baby	48
Lap	96
Twin	168
Double/Queen	232
King	284

2. Select a sharp pencil in a color that will show visibly on the wrong side of your 2 ¾" squares. This fine line should be easily seen as it will be used for a sewing guide.

3. Place a 6" x 6" ruler edge across the diagonal of the square **directly on the corner points. Do not back the ruler off the points to compensate for the width of the marking line. The marked line will be slightly off center creating a slightly smaller triangle**. This accommodates the fold in the pressed seam.

4. Mark the wrong sides of all 2 ¾" squares in this manner. Sharpen your pencil when necessary. Mark each square and stack consistently with the smaller triangle to the same side.

Sewing the Snowball Block

1. Place a stack of light Snowball squares right side up, on point, to the left of your sewing machine. Place a stack of marked Snowball Corners right side down, on point, either to the front or in the keyhole of your machine. **The smaller triangles should be on the right.**

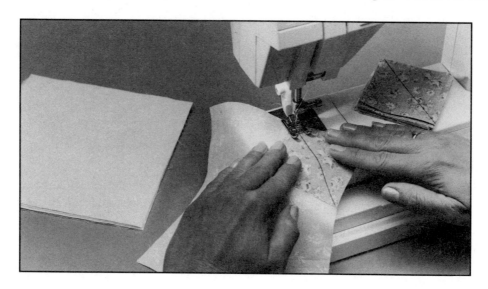

2. With right sides together, place a 2 ¾" square onto the corner of a Snowball square. Position carefully with the smaller triangles touching the outside edges of the snowball square.

3. Position hands on both sides of small square to hold in place while sewing.

4. **Sew directly on the drawn line.** Stop sewing about ½" from the end and position the next block to continue that line. Continue assembly-line sewing a manageable number of blocks. Do not cut connecting threads.

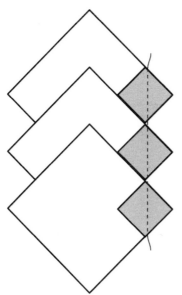 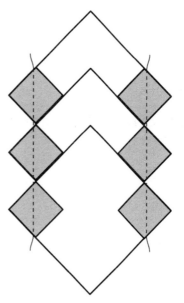

5. Remove from machine and turn around to sew squares on the opposite corner.

6. Carefully cut connecting threads and stack. Sew the remaining two corners in the same manner.

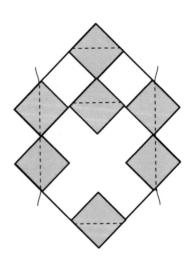

Trimming the Triangles

1. Carefully stack 3 blocks at a time or trim individually.

2. Position the Square Up ruler on the block with its ¼" lines on two upper seams. **Trim corners leaving a ¼" seam allowance.**

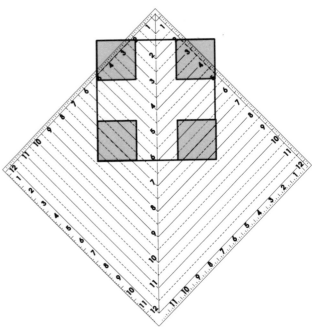

3. Turn block(s) around and trim the remaining two corners.

Pressing the Blocks

1. Place block right side up on ironing board. Press lightly to set the seam.

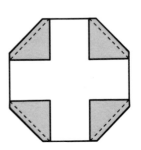

2. Press triangles open. The seam will lie under the triangle.

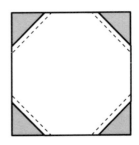

32

Squaring the Snowball Blocks

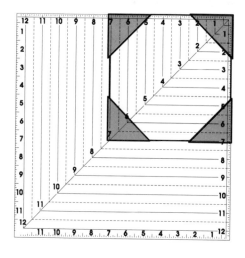

1. Lay a block on the cutting mat. Line up the Square Up ruler with the upper and right edges of the Snowball octagon. Sliver trim the upper and right edges of the triangles.

2. Turn block around. Line up the two remaining sides of the Snowball. Line up inside edges of block with your squared Nine-Patch size that you previously noted on page 27.

   Sliver trim.

Enhancing the Snowball Blocks

You may choose to leave the snowballs plain, or mark a snowflake motif for free motion machine quilting. Another way to add texture without quilting is to sew a 4 to 5 inch doily at the center.

For ease in handling, add doilies or mark for quilting at this time.

Snowflake Stencil Design

Easy-to-use Snowflake design plastic stencil is available from Quilt in a Day.

The snowflake design on page 85 can be centered and traced on the blocks. If the design doesn't show through your fabric, you can use a purchased stencil or make your own. Use a quilter's silver pencil or other easily removed marker.

Free motion machine quilting instructions are found in the Machine Quilting Finish chapter.

Snowflake Doily

Purchase a 4 to 5 inch round lace doily for each snowball block. They can be the same color as the fabric or can contrast.

To keep the doily from shifting, pin through each point.

Use a matching thread to topstitch the outside edge of the doily. Loosen top tension.

To prevent the edges from curling, stitch close to the edge using 10 stitches per inch or #3 on settings numbered from 1 to 4. Pivot at the angles with the needle in the fabric.

Sewing the Blocks Together

Stack an equal number of Nine-Patch and Snowball blocks according to your size quilt. Stack the Nine-Patch blocks with Fabric **1** in the upper left hand corner. The remaining blocks will be used in the right side row.

Number of blocks in each stack:

Baby	10
Lap	21
Twin	36
Double/Queen	52
King	65

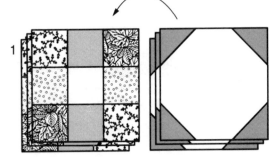

Matching Seams

When sewing a Nine-Patch to a Snowball, the seams will align at the two "match points."

To find your match points, flip a Snowball onto a Nine-Patch. Turn the pair counterclockwise with the side to be sewn on top.

Turn down upper edge of the Snowball to see seams. If necessary, shift block to align the seams at the two "match points."

Due to varying seam allowances, your match points might not be exactly ¼" from the edge. Find your match points along the diagonal line, slightly more or less than ¼". **The width of your seam allowance is determined by your match points.**

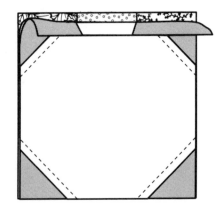

To Pin or Not to Pin

The pinning process results in well matched seams. You may, however, choose to disregard the pinning instructions because pinning is time consuming. Blocks that have been consistently sewn and squared may not require match pinning. If you start sewing the blocks together without pinning and are not satisfied with the match, you may decide to pin.

Other alternatives to pinning are:

1. Hold the pair up to a light or window to see through the blocks. Shift and center the seams. Sew across the match points.

2. **Fingerpinning:** As you sew towards a seam, lift up the top block to determine the match point. Ease fabric if necessary.

3. **Feeling Technique:** When the Snowball block is on top you can see or feel the seams underneath to determine the match points.

If not pinning: Skip to "Sewing Pairs of Snowball/Nine-Patch Blocks."

Match Pinning Snowball to Nine-Patch

1. While pinning, position the stack of Snowball blocks above the Nine-Patch stack. Turn the Nine-Patch stack with Fabric **1** positioned in the lower left corner.

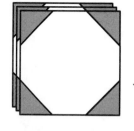

2. Flip a Snowball block down onto the Nine-Patch.

3. Turn down upper edge of the Snowball block to align the seams at the two match points.

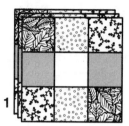

4. Place a pin in the diagonal seam at the match point, approximately ¼" from the edge. **Pin through the single layer side of seam, not the seam allowance.**

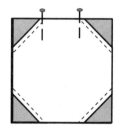

5. Aim the pin at the nine-patch seam. Pin through the single layer side of the seam. Pinch the two blocks together to avoid shifting when the pin is set.

6. Pin the second "match point" of that pair.

7. Flip the pinned pair to the right and continue match pinning pairs.

8. Turn the stack over with the first pair on top and "match pins" on right.

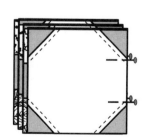

Sewing Pairs of Snowball/Nine-Patch Blocks

Unpinned

If not pinning, flip Snowball onto Nine-Patch.

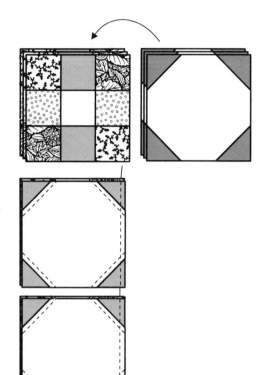

Pinning or not pinning

1. Assembly-line sew the pairs. If pinned, sew through the match points, removing pins as you come to them.

If seams do not match, you may improve the alignment by changing the seam allowance.

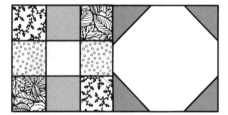   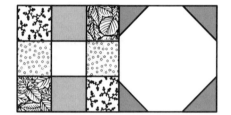

Take deeper seam allowance   Take less seam allowance

2. Clip the connecting threads.

3. Press seams away from Snowball blocks.

4. Open and lay in two equal stacks in opposite directions.

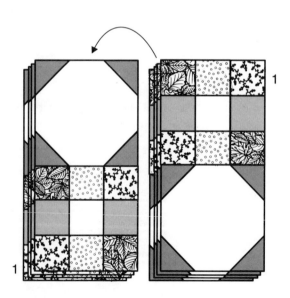

Number of pairs in each stack:

Baby	4
Lap	9
Twin	18
Double/Queen	24
King	30

Depending on your size quilt, there will be extra pairs and single blocks. Twin size does not have extra pairs.

Sewing Pairs into Sets of Four

1. Flip the pair together.

2. Pin the center seam away from the Snowball blocks. Match pin if desired.

3. Assembly-line sew remaining pairs into sets of four.

4. Clip apart and press seams away from Snowball blocks. Seams will twist in the center of the set.

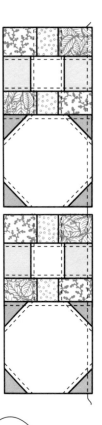

Sewing the Sets Together

1. Lay out the sets according to your size quilt and check the pattern. Always position a Nine-Patch with Fabric **1** in the upper left corner.

Sets across by sets down

Baby	2 x 2
Lap	3 x 3
Twin	3 x 6
Double/Queen	4 x 6
King	5 x 6

2. Flip **vertical row 2** onto **vertical row 1.**

Row 1   Row 2   Row 3

Lap Size Quilt

3. Stack paired rows **1** and **2** with first pair on top.

4. Stack remaining vertical rows.

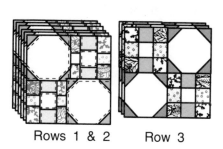

Rows 1 & 2   Row 3

5. Assembly-line sew the first paired stack. Do not clip connecting threads.

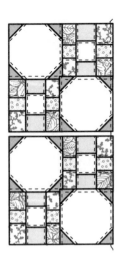

6. For quilt sizes larger than Baby, add remaining stacks in the same manner.

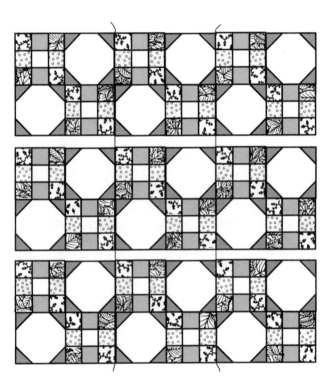

7. Sew the **horizontal** seams by flipping rows together, pinning seams away from the Snowball blocks.

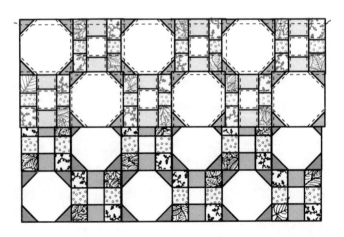

Sewing the Bottom Row

All sizes except twin

1. From remaining pairs, sew into a horizontal row depending on your size quilt.

   Nine-patch will be at the left end of the row with Fabric **1** in the upper left corner.

Example of Lap Size Quilt

Number of pairs for bottom horizontal row

Baby	2
Lap	3
Twin	none
Double/Queen	4
King	5

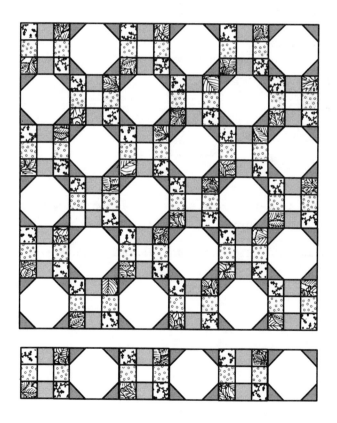

2. Lay out this row with the assembled sets. Check for correct positioning.

3. Sew bottom row, pinning seams away from Snowball blocks.

Sewing the Right Side Row

1. Lay out assembled top with bottom row attached. Lay out the leftover blocks along the right edge, positioning Nine-Patches to extend the pattern. Check block positions to be certain the pattern is laid out correctly.

2. Sew blocks together into a row.

3. Lay row along right side of assembled top. Flip and sew row to the quilt top, pushing seams away from Snowball blocks.

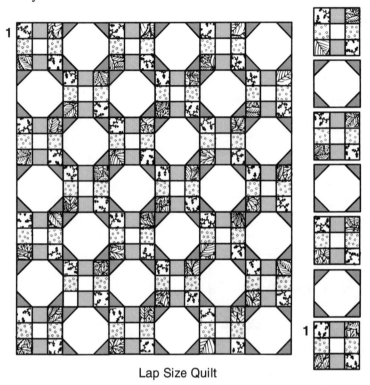

Lap Size Quilt

4. Press quilt top from wrong side first. Either press all seams away from Snowballs (with twisting seams) or press row seams in alternate directions. Press from right side.

5. Place Square Up ruler in corners and sliver trim. Lay long ruler along sides to straighten edges.

Turn to Adding the Borders on page 79.

Fabric Selection for the Star Snowball Quilt

The Star Snowball includes three different Nine-Patches and one Snowball block.

The **Star Block** forms the main body of the star.

1	2	1
2	3	2
1	2	1

The **Chain Blocks** form a connecting chain running diagonally in opposite directions.

3	4	5
4	3	4
5	4	3

At the **Chain Link** the diagonal chains intersect.

3	4	3
4	2	4
3	4	3

The **Snowball** blocks alternate between Nine-Patches. Fabric **1** makes the Star Point, while Fabric **4** is part of the Chain.

First select a multi-colored fabric with two main color families. Use one color family in the star and the second color family in the chain.

Choose a variety of print scales and values. You may follow the recommendations below, or be free to create your own unique design.

	Fabric	Value	Block Position
	1	Dark	Star and Star Points
	2	Medium to Dark	Star and Center of Chain Link
	3	Medium	Center of Chain and Center of Star
	4	Light to Medium	Chain and Snowball Corners
	5	Light	Snowball

Star Snowball Paste Up Sheet

Cut out 1" squares and paste according to fabric number:

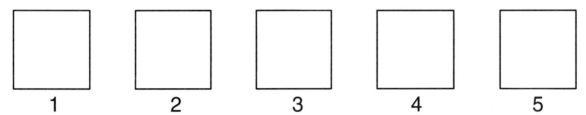

| 1 | 2 | 3 | 4 | 5 |

Star Block

1	2	1
2	3	2
1	2	1

Chain Block

3	4	5
4	3	4
5	4	3

Chain Link

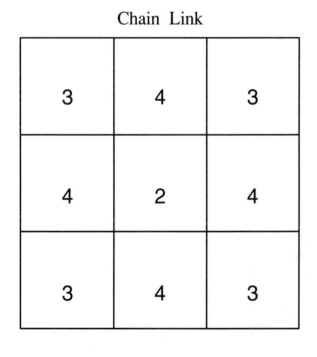

3	4	3
4	2	4
3	4	3

Snowball

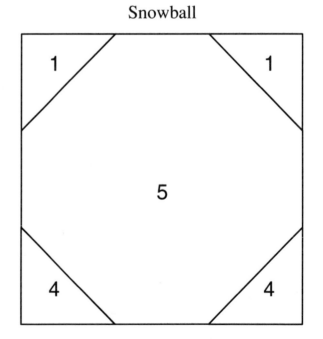

Scrap Variation of the Star Quilt

1. A Star Scrap quilt is shown on the inside front cover. The stars are made in different colors, while the Chain Blocks and Chain Links remain consistent in color. This variation is recommended as your second or third quilt, and must be carefully pre-planned on the layout pages, 76 to 77. Use colored pencils to indicate individual Star colors.

2. Follow yardage chart for your selected size quilt on pages 44 through 50. Do not purchase Fabric **1** and Fabric **2** as listed for Star blocks and Snowball corners. Use scraps to make Star. Start with Fabric **3** and purchase additional fabric as listed.

3. Make the number of Star blocks listed for your size quilt. Make each Star block individually.

To make **one Scrap Star**, cut this many 2 ¾" squares from scraps:

	Nine-Patch	Snowball Corners
Fabric 1	4 squares	8 squares
Fabric 2	4 squares	
Fabric 3	1 square	

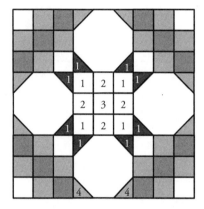

Some Stars are positioned along the outside edge of quilt and may require only six Snowball corner squares. Look at your layout to determine how many Snowball corners are needed for each Star color.

4. Follow instructions for making one Star block on page 51.

5. **Snowball blocks**: Each Snowball block will have two squares of Fabric **4** on one side and two squares of Scrap Fabric **1** on the opposite side. Sew 2 ¾" corner squares following instructions on page 67. Before assembly-line sewing, divide each scrap color into two equal stacks. Use one stack for each side of the block.

6. Make Chain Blocks and Chain Links consistent, as instructed for Star Snowball Quilt.

7. Before sewing blocks together, lay out carefully as planned.

Yardage and Cutting Charts

Star Wallhanging

9 Blocks: 3 across x 3 down
Approximate Finished Size 32" x 32"

1 Star Block
4 Chain Blocks
4 Snowballs

Fabric 1			
Dark	⅓ yd	Star, Snowball Corners	Cut (1) strip, 2 ¾" x 44" into (12) 2 ¾" squares
		First Border	Cut (2) strips, 2" x 44"
Fabric 2			
Medium to Dark	⅛ yd	Star	Cut (4) 2 ¾" squares
Fabric 3			
Medium	¼ yd	Chain	Cut (2) strips, 2 ¾" x 44" cut (1) strip in half
		Center of Star	Cut (1) 2 ¾" square from half strip
Fabric 4			
Light to Medium	⅓ yd	Chain	Cut (2) strips, 2 ¾" x 44" cut (1) strip in half
		Snowball Corners	Cut (1) strip, 2 ¾" x 44" into (8) 2 ¾" squares
Fabric 5			
Light	⅝ yd	Chain	Cut (1) strip, 2 ¾" x 44"
		Snowball	Cut (4) squares later
		Second Border	Cut (4) strips, 1¼" x 25"
Third Border			
	⅝ yd		Cut (2) strips, 4" x 27"
			Cut (2) strips, 4" x 34"
Binding			
	⅜ yd		Cut (3) strips, 3" x 44"
Backing			
	1 yd		
Batting			
	34" x 34"		

Star Baby Quilt

25 Blocks: 5 across x 5 down
Additional Star Point Border
Approximate Finished Size 50" x 50"

5 Star Blocks
4 Chain Links
4 Chain Blocks
12 Snowballs

■ Fabric 1			
Dark	½ yd	Star	Cut (2) strips, 2 ¾" x 44"
		Snowball Corners	Cut (2) strips, 2 ¾" x 44" into (24) 2 ¾" squares
■ Fabric 2			
Medium to Dark	⅓ yd	Star and Center of Chain Link	Cut (3) strips, 2 ¾" x 44" cut (2) strips in half
■ Fabric 3			
Medium	½ yd	Chain and Center of Star	Cut (4) strips, 2 ¾" x 44" cut (1) strip in half
■ Fabric 4			
Light to Medium	⅔ yd	Chain	Cut (4) strips, 2 ¾" x 44" cut (2) strips in half
		Snowball Corners	Cut (2) strips, 2 ¾" x 44" into (24) 2 ¾" squares
□ Fabric 5			
Light, at least 44" wide	1 ¼ yds	Chain	Cut (1) strip, 2 ¾" x 44"
		Snowball	Cut (12) squares later
		Second Border (optional)	Cut (4) strips, 1 ½" x 44"
■ First Border			
	⅜ yd		Cut (4) strips, 2 ½" x 44"
■ Third Border			
	¾ yd		Cut (5) strips, 4 ½" x 44"
Binding			
	⅝ yd		Cut (5) strips, 3" x 44"
Backing			
	3 ⅛ yds		Cut (2) equal pieces
Batting			
	54" x 54"		

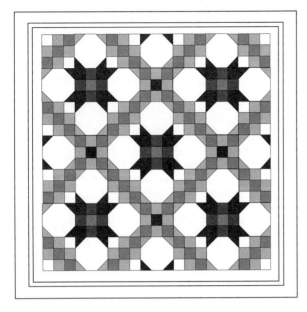

Star Lap Quilt

49 Blocks: 7 across x 7 down
Approximate Finished Size 58" x 58"

5 Star Blocks
4 Chain Links
16 Chain Blocks
24 Snowballs

■ Fabric 1			
Dark	⅝ yd	Star Snowball Corners	Cut (2) strips, 2 ¾" x 44" Cut (4) strips, 2 ¾" x 44" into (48) 2 ¾" squares
■ Fabric 2			
Medium to Dark	⅓ yd	Star and Center of Chain Link	Cut (3) strips, 2 ¾" x 44" cut (2) strips in half
■ Fabric 3			
Medium	⅝ yd	Chain and Center of Star	Cut (6) strips, 2 ¾" x 44" cut (1) strip in half
■ Fabric 4			
Light to Medium	1 yd	Chain	Cut (6) strips, 2 ¾" x 44" cut (1) strip in half
		Snowball Corners	Cut (4) strips, 2 ¾" x 44" into (48) 2 ¾" squares
□ Fabric 5			
Light, at least 44" wide	1 ⅜ yds	Chain Snowball Second Border (optional)	Cut (2) strips, 2 ¾" x 44" Cut (24) squares later Cut (5) strips, 1 ½" x 44"
■ First Border			
Dark	⅜ yd		Cut (5) strips, 2" x 44"
■ Third Border			
Medium	1 yd		Cut (6) strips, 4 ½" x 44"
Binding			
	⅝ yd		Cut (6) strips, 3" x 44"
Backing			
	3 ¾ yds		Cut (2) equal pieces
Batting			
	62" x 62"		

Star Twin Quilt

91 Blocks: 7 across x 13 down
Approximate Finished Size 64" x 102"

10 Star Blocks
11 Chain Links
24 Chain Blocks
46 Snowballs

■ Fabric 1

| Dark | 1 yd | Star | Cut (4) strips, 2 ¾" x 44" |
| | | Snowball Corners | Cut (7) strips, 2 ¾" x 44" into (92) 2 ¾" squares |

■ Fabric 2

| Medium to Dark | ½ yd | Star and Center of Chain Link | Cut (5) strips, 2 ¾" x 44" |

■ Fabric 3

| Medium | 1 yd | Chain and Center of Star | Cut (11) strips, 2 ¾" x 44" |

■ Fabric 4

| Light to Medium | 1 ⅔ yds | Chain Snowball Corners | Cut (12) strips, 2 ¾" x 44" Cut (7) strips, 2 ¾" x 44" into (92) 2 ¾" squares |

□ Fabric 5

| Light, at least 44" wide | 2 ⅓ yds | Chain Snowball | Cut (4) strips, 2 ¾" x 44" Cut (46) squares later |

■ First Border

| Medium to Dark | 1 yd | | Cut (7) strips, 4" x 44" |

□ Second Border

| Light | ⅝ yd | | Cut (8) strips, 2" x 44" |

■ Third Border

| Medium | 1 ⅔ yds | | Cut (9) strips, 6" x 44" |

Binding

| | ⅞ yd | | Cut (9) strips, 3" x 44" |

Backing

| | 6 ½ yds | | Cut (2) equal pieces |

Batting

| | 70" x 108" | | |

Star Double Quilt

117 Blocks: 9 across x 13 down
Approximate Finished Size 80" x 104"

17 Star Blocks
18 Chain Links
24 Chain Blocks
58 Snowballs

■ **Fabric 1**			
Dark	1 ⅜ yds	Star Snowball Corners	Cut (6) strips, 2 ¾" x 44" Cut (8) strips, 2 ¾" x 44" into (116) 2 ¾" squares
■ **Fabric 2**			
Medium to Dark	¾ yd	Star and Center of Chain Link	Cut (8) strips, 2 ¾" x 44" cut (2) strips in half
■ **Fabric 3**			
Medium	1 ⅓ yds	Chain and Center of Star	Cut (14) strips, 2 ¾" x 44" cut (1) strip in half
■ **Fabric 4**			
Light to Medium	2 yds	Chain Snowball Corners	Cut (14) strips, 2 ¾" x 44" cut (1) strip in half Cut (8) strips, 2 ¾" x 44" into (116) 2 ¾" squares
□ **Fabric 5**			
Light, at least 44" wide	2 ¾ yds	Chain Snowball	Cut (4) strips, 2 ¾" x 44" Cut (58) squares later
■ **First Border**			
Medium to Dark	1 yd		Cut (8) strips, 3 ½" x 44"
□ **Second Border**			
Light	1 ¼ yds		Cut (8) strips, 4 ½" x 44"
■ **Third Border**			
Medium	1 ⅞ yds		Cut (9) strips, 6 ½" x 44"
Binding			
	1 yd		Cut (9) strips, 3" x 44"
Backing			
	7 yds		Cut (2) equal pieces
Batting			
	86" x 110"		

48

Star Queen Quilt

117 Blocks: 9 across x 13 down
Approximate Finished Size 86" x 110"

17 Star Blocks
18 Chain Links
24 Chain Blocks
58 Snowballs

■ **Fabric 1**			
Dark	1 ⅜ yds	Star	Cut (6) strips, 2 ¾" x 44"
		Snowball Corners	Cut (8) strips, 2 ¾" x 44" into (116) 2 ¾" squares
■ **Fabric 2**			
Medium to Dark	¾ yd	Star and Center of Chain Link	Cut (8) strips, 2 ¾" x 44" cut (2) strips in half
■ **Fabric 3**			
Medium	1 ⅓ yds	Chain and Center of Star	Cut (14) strips, 2 ¾" x 44" cut (1) strip in half
▧ **Fabric 4**			
Light to Medium	2 yds	Chain	Cut (14) strips, 2 ¾" x 44" cut (1) strip in half
		Snowball Corners	Cut (8) strips, 2 ¾" x 44" into (116) 2 ¾" squares
□ **Fabric 5**			
Light, at least 44" wide	2 ¾ yds	Chain	Cut (4) strips, 2 ¾" x 44"
		Snowball	Cut (58) squares later
■ **First Border**			
Medium to Dark	1 ⅛ yds		Cut (8) strips, 4 ½" x 44"
□ **Second Border**			
Light	1 ⅜ yds		Cut (8) strips, 5 ½" x 44"
▨ **Third Border**			
Medium	2 ¼ yds		Cut (9) strips, 7 ½" x 44"
Binding			
	1 yd		Cut (10) strips, 3" x 44"
Backing			
	8 ½ yds		Cut (3) equal pieces
Batting			
	94" x 116"		

Star King Quilt

143 Blocks: 11 across x 13 down
Approximate Finished Size 96" x 108"

17 Star Blocks
18 Chain Links
36 Chain Blocks
72 Snowballs

■ **Fabric 1**			
Dark	1 ½ yds	Star	Cut (6) strips, 2 ¾" x 44"
		Snowball Corners	Cut (10) strips, 2 ¾" x 44"
			into (144) 2 ¾" squares
■ **Fabric 2**			
Medium to Dark	⅞ yd	Star and	Cut (8) strips, 2 ¾" x 44"
		Center of Chain Link	cut (2) strips in half
▨ **Fabric 3**			
Medium	1 ⅜ yds	Chain and	Cut (15) strips, 2 ¾" x 44"
		Center of Star	cut (1) strip in half
▨ **Fabric 4**			
Light to Medium	2 ⅓ yds	Chain	Cut (16) strips, 2 ¾" x 44"
			cut (2) strips in half
		Snowball Corners	Cut (10) strips, 2 ¾" x 44"
			into (144) 2 ¾" squares
☐ **Fabric 5**			
Light, at least 44" wide	3 ¼ yds	Chain	Cut (5) strips, 2 ¾" x 44"
		Snowball	Cut (72) squares later
■ **First Border**			
Medium to Dark	1 yd		Cut (8) strips, 3 ½" x 44"
☐ **Second Border**			
Light	1 ½ yds		Cut (9) strips, 5 ½" x 44"
▨ **Third Border**			
Medium	2 ¼ yds		Cut (10) strips, 7" x 44"
Binding			
	1 yd		Cut (10) strips, 3" x 44"
Backing			
	9 yds		Cut (3) equal pieces
Batting			
	102" x 114"		

Star Snowball Quilt

 Making One Star Block

Wallhanging or Star Scrap only

All other sizes turn to next page.

1. Count out this many 2 ¾" squares:

Fabric 1	4 squares
Fabric 2	4 squares
Fabric 3	1 square

2. Arrange your squares in this order:

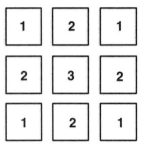

3. Assembly-line sew **vertical** rows using an accurate ¼" seam allowance.

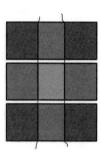

4. Press seams as illustrated:

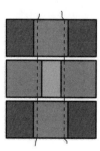

5. Sew **horizontal** seams by flipping rows together and matching seams.

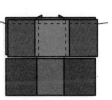

6. Turn to "Making the Chain Block" on page 58.

Making the Star Blocks

All sizes larger than wallhanging.

Make this many blocks:

Baby	5
Lap	5
Twin	10
Double/Queen	17
King	17

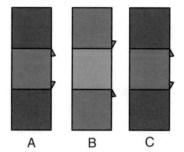

A   B   C

The completed block is made of Section A, B, and C. Sections A and C are identical and are made at the same time.

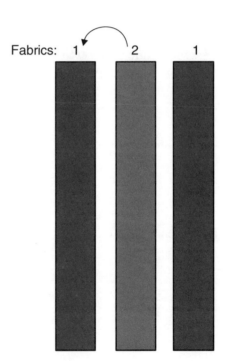 Making Sections A and C

1. Arrange this many 2 ¾" strips in each stack:

Number of strips per stack

Baby	1
Lap	1
Twin	2
Double/Queen	3
King	3

Fabrics: 1   2   1

2. Flip a strip **2** onto **1**, right sides together.

3. Set your machine to 15 stitches per inch, or 2 to 2.5 on machines with stitch selection from 1 to 4.

4. Sew a few inches with an accurate ¼" seam allowance.

   Stop sewing and measure the seam. Make an adjustment if necessary. An accurate, consistent seam allowance is critical to the assembly of the block. Seams will match better and your unfinished block will square up to 7".

5. For larger quilts, assembly-line sew the strips together by butting one pair of strips after the other. Do not raise the presser foot or clip the threads.

6. Flip **1** onto **2** and sew right sides together.

   For larger quilts, assembly-line sew all strips from the stack.

7. **Baby and Lap**. Cut the section in half. Label Sections A and C. Set aside.

   Twin, Double/Queen, and King. Clip connecting threads.

   Double/Queen and King: Cut one section in half. Divide the sections equally in half. Label Sections A and C. Set aside.

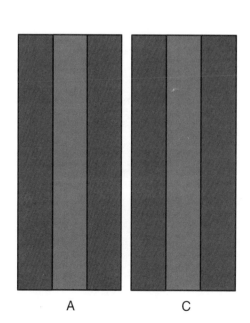

A   C

You will have this many strip lengths for Sections A and C:

Baby/Lap	½ strip
Twin	1 strip
Double/Queen/King	1 ½ strips

Making Section B

1. Arrange this many 2 ¾" strips in each stack.

Number of strips per stack:

Baby	1 half-strip
Lap	1 half-strip
Twin	1 strip
Double/Queen	1 strip/1 half-strip
King	1 strip/1 half-strip

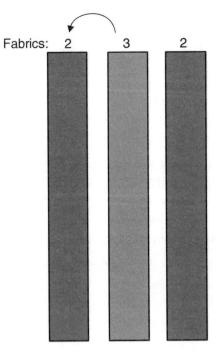

Fabrics: 2 3 2

2. Sew the strips together as before.

3. Clip connecting threads. Label Section B.
   You will have the same number of strip
   lengths as for Sections A and C.

4. Press seams of Sections A and C away from
   the center.

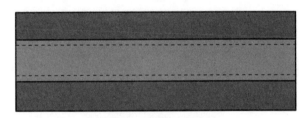

Sections A and C

5. Press seams of Section B toward the center.

   Press out any folds in seams.

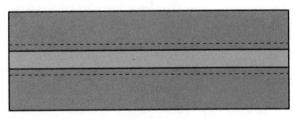

Section B

54

Cutting Sections A and B

1. Place Section A **right side up** on the cutting mat.

2. Place Section B right sides together onto Section A. Carefully line up the top and left edges. Run your hand along the seams to interlock them.

3. With the 6" x 12" ruler and rotary cutter, square off the left edge to straighten and remove the selvage.

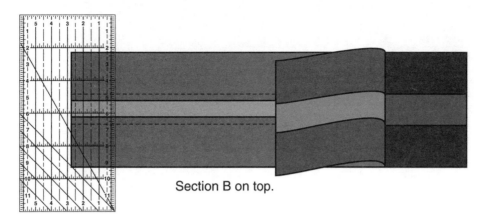

Section B on top.

4. Use the ruler lines to measure in 2 ¾", and cut the paired pieces.

5. For accurate cutting, line up one of the horizontal ruler lines with a fabric strip below. This will prevent your cuts from running off angle. Make straightening cuts if you lose that right angle.

6. Layer cut every 2 ¾", carefully lifting, moving, and lining up the ruler. You should cut 15 pairs from each layered section.

7. As you cut each pair, carefully place it onto a large plexiglass ruler for convenience in carrying the pieces to the sewing machine.

8. Cut this many pairs:

Baby	5
Lap	5
Twin	10
Double/Queen	17
King	17

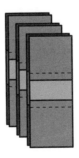

Note: Most sewers will get 15 cuts across. If you have short strips or cutting errors, you may need to assemble more shorter sections to get your required number. Allowance has been given in the yardage charts.

9. Label the pairs A/B.

Cutting Section C

1. Place Section C on the cutting mat right side up. Square off the left edge to straighten and remove the selvage. Cut the pieces every 2 ¾". Cut through single thickness only.

2. Cut and stack the same number of pieces as paired A/B listed according to your quilt size. Label the stack C.

Cut this many pieces

Baby	5
Lap	5
Twin	10
Double/Queen	17
King	17

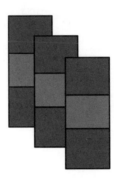

Sewing the Sections Together

Sections A and B

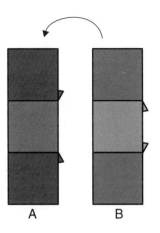

1. Flip open one of the paired pieces to check for proper arrangement of strips. Turn to correct if necessary.

2. Pick up a paired piece A/B and line up the first seams interlocking with one seam up and the other seam down.

   Fingerpinning:
   Hold your finger over the seam as you approach it. Once sewn, line up the second seams, stretching to meet if necessary. Again place your finger over the second seam as it is approached.

3. Assembly-line sew by butting one pair after the other.

   Sew all paired A/B in the stack. Do not clip connecting threads.

Adding Section C

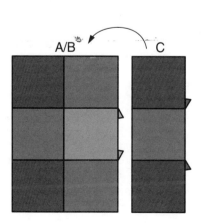

1. Beginning with the first A/B pair, open and position next to a Section C piece. Check for proper arrangement.

2. Assembly-line sew as before.

3. Press seams away from center. Press from both the right and wrong sides to press out any folds in the seams.

Making the Chain Blocks

Make this many blocks:

Wallhanging	4
Baby	4
Lap	16
Twin	24
Double/Queen	24
King	36

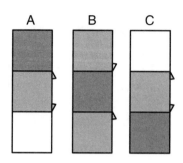

 Making Sections A and C

1. Arrange this many 2 ¾" strips in each stack:

Number of strips per stack

Wallhanging	1
Baby	1
Lap	2
Twin	4
Double/Queen	4
King	5

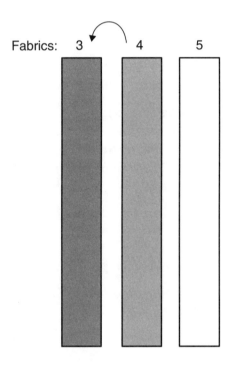

Fabrics: 3 4 5

2. Sew strips together as before.

3. **Wallhanging, Baby and King size**: Cut one section in half. Label Sections A and C. Set aside.

4. **Lap, Twin, Double/Queen and King size**: Divide the sections equally in half. Label Sections A and C. Set aside.

You will have this many strip lengths for Sections A and C:

Wallhanging/Baby	½ strip
Lap	1 strip
Twin/Double/Queen	2 strips
King	2 ½ strips

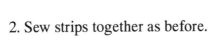 Making Section B

1. Arrange this many 2 ¾" strips in each stack:

Fabrics: 4 3 4

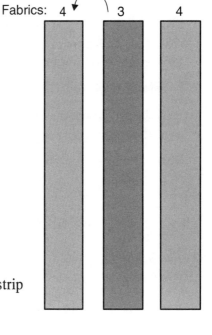

Number of strips per stack:

Wallhanging	1 half-strip
Baby	1 half-strip
Lap	1
Twin	2
Double/Queen	2
King	2 strips/1 half-strip

2. Sew strips together as before.

3. Label Section B. You will have the same number of strip lengths as for Sections A and C.

4. **Press seams of Section B away from the center.**

5. **Press seams of Sections A and C toward the center.**

Cutting Sections A and B

1. Place Section A **right side up** on the cutting mat with **Fabric 3 across the top edge.** For sizes larger than lap, always position Section A with Fabric **3** across the top edge.

2. Place Section B right sides together onto Section A. Carefully line up the strips and cut 2 ¾" paired pieces as before.

   Wallhanging: Refer to cutting instructions on page 55.

3. Cut this many pairs:

Wallhanging	4
Baby	4
Lap	15
Twin	24
Double/Queen	24
King	36

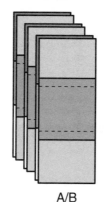

A/B

4. Label the pairs A/B.

Cutting Section C

1. Place Section C **right side up** on the cutting mat with **Fabric 5 across the top edge**. Cut the same number of 2 ¾" pieces as for the paired A/B.

2. Label the stack C.

   Lap Quilt: Make one more block to get the required number (16) for your quilt.

   Refer to making one block on page 51.

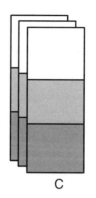

C

Sewing the Sections Together

Sections A and B

1. Flip open one of the paired pieces to check for proper arrangement of strips. Correct if necessary.

2. Assembly-line sew all paired A/B as before.

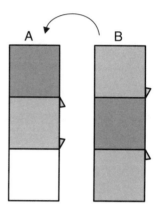

Adding Section C

1. Lay out a C piece next to the paired A/B.

   Section C should be turned around from the position of Section A. Correct if necessary.

2. Assembly-line sew all pieces from the C stack.

3. Clip connecting threads.

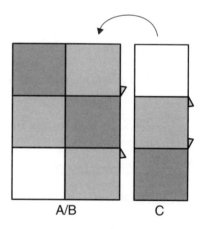

A/B   C

4. Press the seams toward the center.

   Wallhanging: Turn to Squaring Nine-Patches on page 63.

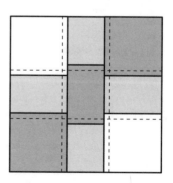

Making the Chain Link

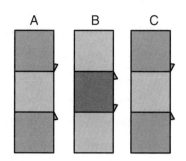

Make this many blocks:

Baby	4
Lap	4
Twin	11
Double/Queen	18
King	18

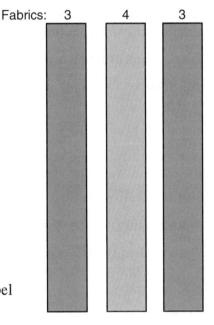 Making Sections A and C

1. Arrange this many 2 ¾" strips in each stack:

Number of strips per stack

Baby	1
Lap	1
Twin	2
Double/Queen	3
King	3

2. Sew strips together as before.

3. **Baby and Lap size:** Cut the section in half. Label the Sections A and C. Set aside.

4. **Double/Queen and King size:** Cut one section in half.

5. Divide the sections equally in half. Label Sections A and C. Set Aside.

You will have this many strip lengths for Sections A and C:

Baby/Lap	½ strip
Twin	1 strip
Double/Queen/King	1 ½ strips

Making Section B

1. Arrange this many 2 ¾" strips in each stack:

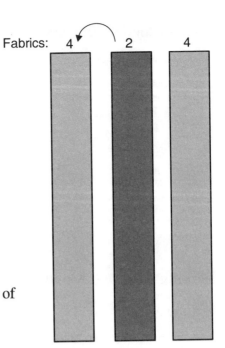

Fabrics: 4 2 4

Number of strips per stack

Baby	1 half-strip
Lap	1 half-strip
Twin	1 strip
Double/queen	1 strip/1 half-strip
King	1 strip/1 half-strip

2. Sew strips together as before.

3. Label Section B. You will have the same number of strip lengths as for Sections A and C.

4. **Press seams of Section B toward the center.**

5. **Press seams of Sections A and C away from the center.**

Cutting Sections A and B

1. **Place Section A right side up on the cutting mat.**

2. Place Section B right sides together onto Section A. Carefully line up the strips and cut 2 ¾" paired pieces as before.

3. Cut this many pairs for your quilt:

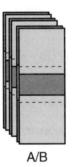

A/B

Baby	4
Lap	4
Twin	11
Double/Queen	18
King	18

Cutting Section C

Place Section C on the cutting mat and cut the same number of 2 ¾" pieces as for the paired A/B.

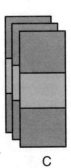

C

Sewing the Sections Together

Sections A and B

1. Flip open one of the paired pieces to check for proper arrangement of strips. Turn to correct if necessary.

2. Assembly-line sew all paired A/B as before.

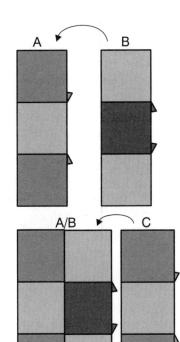

Adding Section C

1. Lay out a C piece next to the paired A/B to check for proper arrangement of the strips. Turn to correct if necessary.

2. Assembly-line sew all pieces from the C stack.

3. Clip connecting threads.

4. Press the seams away from the center.

Squaring Nine-Patches

1. Using a Square Up ruler, measure several blocks to find an average size. **In most cases, the blocks will square up to 7".**

2. If your blocks measure slightly ($1/8$") over 7" square, square them to 7". Your blocks may all square to 7 $1/8$" or 6 $7/8$" depending on your seam allowance. **(Do not trim off more than $1/8$"from any one side.)** Over trimming may create problems later when matching seams.

3. First Trim: Position the diagonal line of the ruler to cross the matched center seams. Center your squaring size measurement, for example 7". Look at all four sides in order to trim equally.

   Sliver trim the right and top edges of the block.

4. Second Trim: Turn the block around with the two trimmed edges lining up on your squaring size, for example 7".

   Sliver trim the two remaining edges of the block.

5. Record the size of your squared Nine Patches: _____

Star Snowball Blocks

Cutting the Light Strips

The fabric should measure at least 44" from selvage to selvage in order to get 6 generous 7" squares across a width. Yardage allows one extra strip for cutting errors.

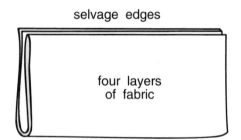

selvage edges

four layers of fabric

1. Place your light snowball fabric on the cutting mat with the fold at the bottom. Line up the two selvage edges along the entire length of the fabric.

2. Bring the folded edge up to line up with the selvage edges. Carefully line up the entire length of the fabric to avoid crooked strips.

3. Place the Square Up ruler along the left edge of the fabric. Line up the top edge of the ruler with the selvage/fold. Square off the left edge of the fabric, being careful to cut through all four thicknesses.

   By working on the left corner of a table, you can square off by moving to the left side of the table. Stand in front of the table while cutting strips.

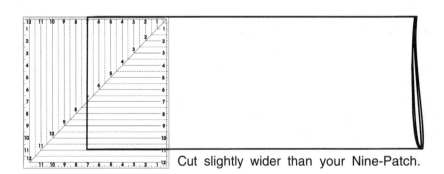

Cut slightly wider than your Nine-Patch.

4. Because the Snowball Block "shrinks" slightly after the corners are sewn, the **light strips are cut slightly wider than your Nine-Patch measurement**. Look at the inch lines on your quilting ruler. **Add the width of the ruler line to the size of your Nine-Patch**.

Cut this many strips:

Wallhanging	1
Baby	2
Lap	4
Twin	8
Double/Queen	10
King	12

As you cut your strips, unfold and check periodically for straightness. Straighten the left edge when necessary.

Cutting The Snowball Squares

1. With the square ruler, square off the left edge of the folded strip to straighten and remove the selvages. Check left edge to be certain you are cutting through two layers.

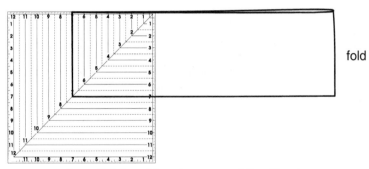

fold

Cut slightly wider than your Nine-Patch.

2. Use the ruler lines to measure in your strip width (for example, 7" plus width of ruler line). For all sizes larger than wallhanging: **Cut six squares per strip.**

Cut this many squares:

Wallhanging	4
Baby	12
Lap	24
Twin	46
Double/Queen	58
King	72

Marking the Snowball Corners

1. Count out this many 2 ¾" squares:

	Fabric 1	Fabric 4
Wallhanging	8	8
Baby	24	24
Lap	48	48
Twin	92	92
Double/Queen	116	116
King	144	144

2. Select a sharp pencil in a color that will show visibly on the wrong side of your 2 ¾" squares. This fine line should be easily seen as it will be used for a sewing guide.

3. Place a 6" x 6" ruler edge across the diagonal of the square **directly on the corner points. Do not back the ruler off the points to compensate for the width of the marking line. The marked line will be slightly off center creating a slightly smaller triangle.** This accommodates the fold in the pressed seam .

4. Mark the wrong sides of all 2 ¾" squares in this manner. Sharpen your pencil when necessary. Mark each square and stack consistently with the smaller triangle to the same side.

Layout of the Snowball Block

The Star quilt uses two squares of Fabric **1** (Star Points) on one side, and uses two squares of Fabric **4** (Chain) on the opposite side.

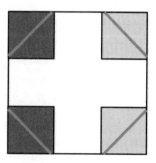

Sewing the Snowball Block

1. Place a stack of light Snowball squares right side up, on point, to the left of your sewing machine. Place a stack of marked Snowball Corners, Fabric **4**, right side down, on point, either to the front or in the keyhole of your machine. **The smaller triangles should be on the right.** See page 31.

2. With right sides together, place a 2 ¾" square onto the corner of a Snowball square. Position carefully with the smaller triangles touching the outside edges of the snowball square.

3. Position hands on both sides of small square to hold in place while sewing.

4. **Sew directly on the drawn line.** Stop sewing about ½" from the end and position the next block to continue that line. Continue assembly-line sewing a manageable number of blocks. Do not cut connecting threads.

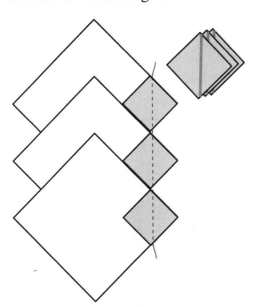 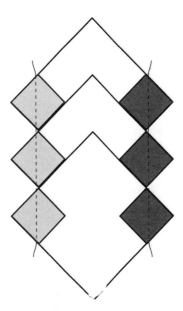

5. Remove from machine and turn around to sew squares on the opposite corner.

6. **Use your other Fabric 1 on the opposite corner.**

7. Carefully cut connecting threads and stack. Sew the remaining two corners in the same manner.

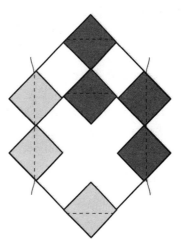

Trimming the Triangles

1. Carefully stack 3 blocks at a time or trim individually.

2. Position the Square Up ruler on the block with its ¼" lines on two upper seams. **Trim corners leaving a ¼" seam allowance.**

3. Turn block(s) around and trim the remaining two corners.

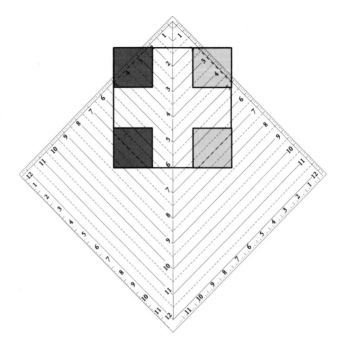

Pressing the Blocks

Place block right side up on ironing board. Press lightly to set the seam. Press triangles open. The seam will lie under the triangle

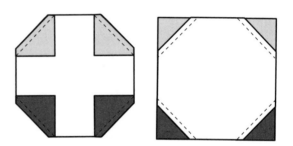

Squaring the Snowball Blocks

1. Lay a block on the cutting mat. Line up the Square Up ruler with the upper and right edges of the Snowball octagon. Sliver trim the upper and right edges of the triangles.

2. Turn block around. Line up the two remaining sides of the Snowball. Line up inside edges of block with your squared Nine-Patch size on page 63. Sliver trim.

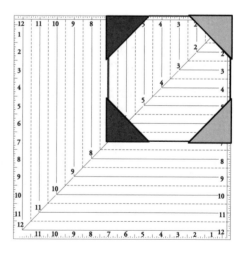

Enhancing the Snowball Blocks

You may choose to leave the snowballs plain, or mark a snowflake motif for free motion machine quilting. Another way to add texture without quilting is to sew a 4 to 5 inch doily at the center. For detailed instructions see page 33.

Sewing the Blocks Together

The Star Quilts are assembled from smaller units called "sets." The sets are made from different numbers of blocks depending on your size quilt.

Making Sets of Nine

1. Count out this many blocks:

	Star Blocks	Chain Blocks	Snowballs
Wallhanging	1	4	4
Baby	1	4	4
Lap	4	16	16
Twin	6	24	24
Double/Queen	4	16	16
King	9	36	36

Reserve remaining Star Blocks for Sewing Sets Together.

2. Lay out and stack blocks:

Check to be certain all blocks are turned correctly.

Number of blocks per stack:

Wallhanging/Baby	1
Lap	4
Twin	6
Double/Queen	4
King	9

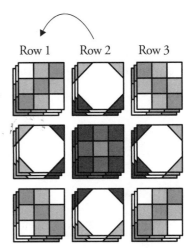

Row 1   Row 2   Row 3

Matching Seams

When sewing a Nine-Patch to a Snowball, the seams will align at the two "match points".

To find your match points, flip a Snowball onto a Nine-Patch. Turn the pair counterclockwise with the side to be sewn on top.

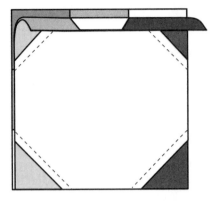

Turn down upper edge of the Snowball to see seams. If necessary, shift block to align the seams at the two "match points."

Due to varying seam allowances, your match points might not be exactly ¼" from the edge. Find your match points along the diagonal line, slightly more or less than ¼". **The width of your seam allowance is determined by your match points.**

To Pin or Not to Pin

The pinning process results in well matched seams. You may, however, choose not to "match pin" because it is time consuming. Blocks that have been consistently sewn and squared may not require match pinning. Some alternatives to pinning are given on page 34. If you start sewing the blocks together without pinning and are not satisfied with the match, you may decide to pin. **Refer to page 35 for pinning instructions (Steps 4 through 7).**

Making One Set of Nine

Vertical Rows

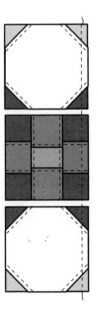

1. Flip **vertical Row 2** right sides together onto **vertical Row 1**.

2. Stack the pairs with the first on top.

3. Assembly-line sew the pairs from the stack. Do not clip the connecting threads.

   If "match pinning", sew through the matched points, removing pins as you come to them.

If seams do not match, you may improve the alignment by changing the seam allowance.

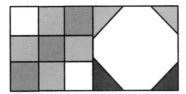
Take deeper seam allowance

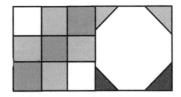
Take less seam allowance

4. For sizes larger than Baby, you may choose to make one set at a time, or assembly-line sew all pairs of the first two vertical rows.

5. Stack Row 3 with the first block on top.

6. Flip and assembly-line sew onto Row 2. For larger quilts, continue assembly-line sewing. Clip connecting threads after every three rows. Press seams away from Snowball blocks.

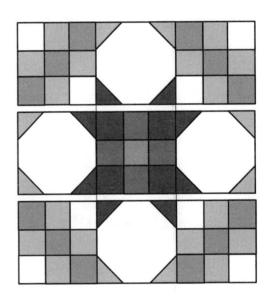

Horizontal Rows

1. Flip first horizontal row right sides together onto second horizontal row.

2. At connecting threads pin the seams away from Snowball blocks.

3. Sew one set at a time or assembly-line sew multiple sets.

   Press from wrong side first. Either press all seams away from Snowballs (with twisting seams) or press row seams in alternate directions. Press from right side.

   Wallhanging only: turn to Adding Borders on page 79.

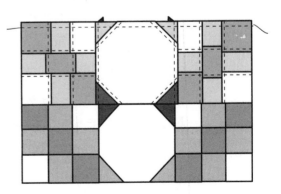

Making Sets of Three

1. Count out this many blocks:

	Chain Links	Snowballs
Baby	4	8
Lap	4	8
Twin	11	22
Double/Queen	12	24
King	18	36

2. Divide the Snowball Blocks into two equal stacks. **Check for correct positioning of blocks. The dark Star Points should be on the outside.**

3. Lay out and stack blocks according to your quilt size.

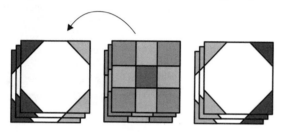

4. Flip the top Chain Link to the left onto the Snowball Block. Sew right sides together.

5. Continue assembly-line sewing all blocks from the first two stacks. If "match pinning," stack pairs, pin and sew as before.

6. Do not clip connecting threads.

7. Flip and assembly-line sew remaining stack of Snowball Blocks.

8. Press seams away from Snowball Blocks.

Lap, Twin and King Sizes only: Turn to Sewing Sets Together on page 78.

Double/Queen only: Turn to Sewing Sets of Six on page 75.

Making Star Point Border for Baby Quilt Only

Light Fabric 5	cut (4) strips, 2 ¾" x 45"	into (20) 2 ¾" x your block size (for example: 7") and (4) 2 ¾" squares for corners
Dark Fabric 1	cut (1) strip, 2 ¾" x 45" plus (1) square	into (16) 2 ¾" squares
Fabric 4	cut (1) strip, 2 ¾" x 45"	into (8) 2 ¾" squares

8  Making Star Points

and

4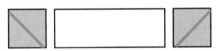

1. As done previously for the Snowball Block corners, mark diagonals across 2 ¾" squares in Fabrics **1** and **4**.

Lay out 8 in each stack   Lay out 4 in each stack

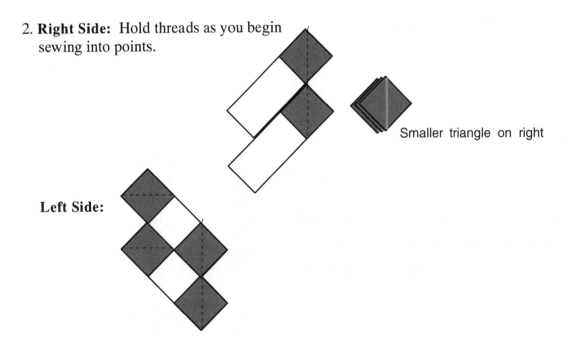

2. **Right Side:** Hold threads as you begin sewing into points.

Smaller triangle on right

Left Side:

3. Trim off smaller triangles leaving ¼" seam allowance.

4. Press open with seam under triangle.

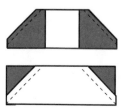

Baby only: Making Four

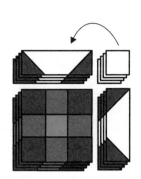

1. Count out four Star Blocks.

2. Divide Star Points Fabric **1** in two equal stacks of four.

3. Lay out with the four light 2 ¾" squares.

4. Assembly-line sew vertical rows.

5. Cut apart every second row.

6. Sew horizontal seams. At connecting threads, press both seams down.

 Making Four

1. Count out eight light strips, 2 ¾" x your block size. Divide into two equal stacks.

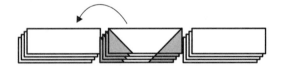

2. Lay out with four Star Points Fabric **4.**

3. Assembly-line sew as before.

4. Press seams toward Star points.

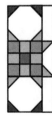

Making Four

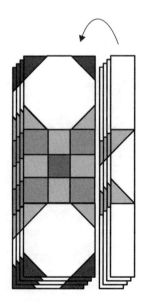

1. Lay out four Star Point strips with four sets of three.

2. Assembly-line sew. Cut connecting threads.

3. Press seams toward Snowball Blocks.

4. Turn to Sewing Sets Together on page 78.

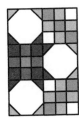

Double/Queen only: Making Four Sets of Six

1. Count out:

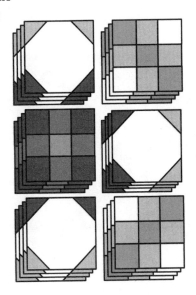

   (4) Star Blocks,

   (8) Chain Blocks, divide into two stack of four

   (12) Snowball Blocks, divide into three stacks of four

2. Lay out stacks. Check for correct positioning of blocks. Assembly-line sew vertical seams. Cut apart after third block.

3. Sew horizontal seams. Clip connecting threads. Press seams away from Snowball Block.

Making Six Sets of Two

1. Stack and lay out:

Position Star Points on outside.

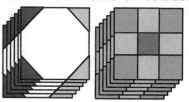

   (6) Snowball Blocks

   (6) Chain Link Blocks

2. Flip right sides together and assembly-line sew all pairs.

3. Clip connecting thread. Press seams away from Snowball blocks.

Lay Out Sets and Blocks

All sizes except Wallhanging: Lay out sets and any remaining Star Blocks according to your size quilt.

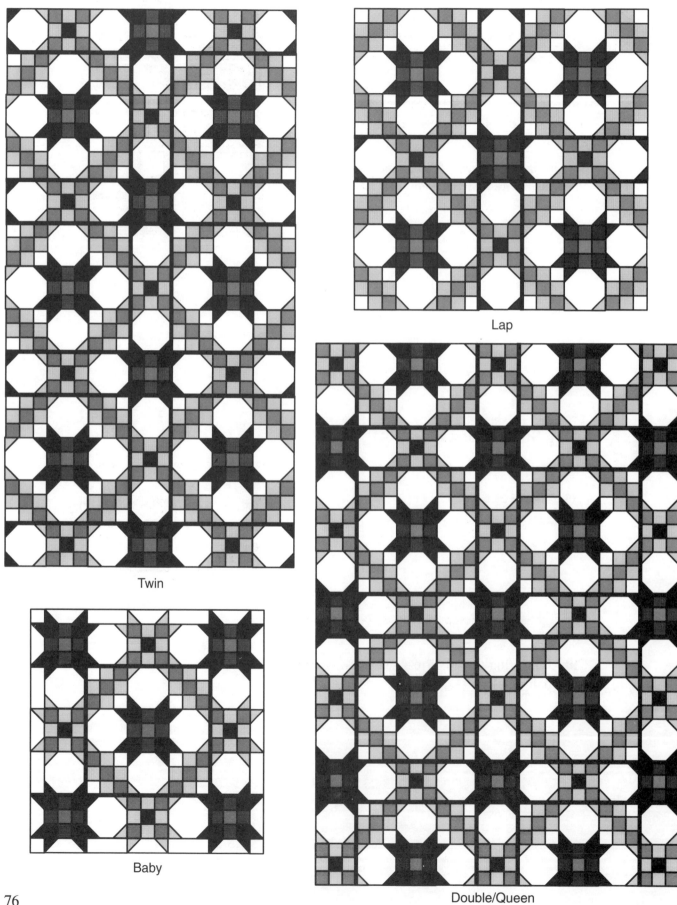

Twin

Lap

Baby

Double/Queen

King

Sewing Sets Together

1. Flip **vertical row 2** onto **vertical row 1**.

2. Stack paired rows **1** and **2** with first pair on top.

3. Stack remaining vertical rows.

4. Assembly-line sew the first two stacks. Do not clip connecting threads.

5. Add remaining stacks in the same manner.

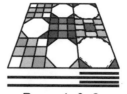

Rows 1 & 2

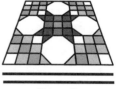

Row 3

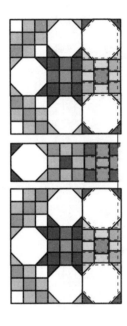

6. Sew the horizontal seams by flipping rows together, pushing seams away from the snowball blocks.

7. Press quilt top from the wrong side first. Either press all seams away from Snowballs (with twisting seams) or press row seams in alternate directions. Press from right side.

8. Place Square Up ruler in corners and sliver-trim. Lay long ruler along sides to straighten edges.

Adding the Borders

Designing Your Borders

Be creative when adding borders. Suggested border yardage and border examples are given for each quilt. However, you may wish to custom design the borders by changing the widths of the strips. This might change backing and batting yardage.

When custom fitting the quilt, lay the top on your bed before adding the borders and backing. Measure to find how much border is needed to get the fit you want. Keep in mind that a large quilt will "shrink" approximately 3" in the length and width after machine quilting.

Piecing Long Borders and Binding Strips

1. Stack and square off the ends of each strip, trimming away the selvage edges.

2. Seam the strips of each fabric into long pieces by assembly-line sewing. Lay the first strip right side up. Lay the second strip right sides to it. Backstitch, stitch the short ends together, and backstitch again.

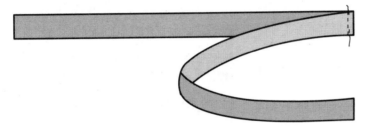

3. Take the strip on the top and fold it so the right side is up.

4. Place the third strip right sides to it, backstitch, stitch, and backstitch again.

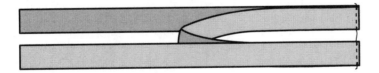

5. Continue assembly-line sewing all the short ends together into long pieces for each fabric.

6. Clip the threads holding the strips together.

7. Press seams to one side.

8. **Press length of binding strip in half, with right side out.**

Sewing the Borders to the Quilt Top

1. Measure down the center to find the length. Cut two side strips that measurement plus two inches.

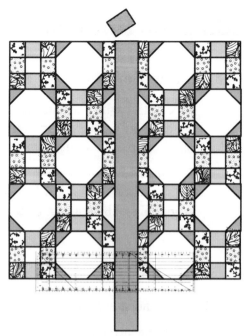

2. Right sides together, match and pin the center of the strips to the center of the sides. Pin at ends, allowing an extra inch of border at each end. Pin every three inches. Sew with the quilt on top in order to see seams.

3. Press seams toward the borders. Square off the ends of the strips.

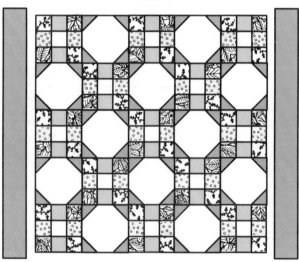

4. Measure the width across the center including newly added borders. Cut two strips that measurement plus two inches.

5. Right sides together, match and pin the center of the strips to the center of the top and bottom edges of the quilt. Pin at the ends, allowing an extra inch of border at both ends. Pin every three inches. Sew with the quilt on top.

6. Press seams toward the borders. Square off the corners.

Repeat these steps for additional borders.

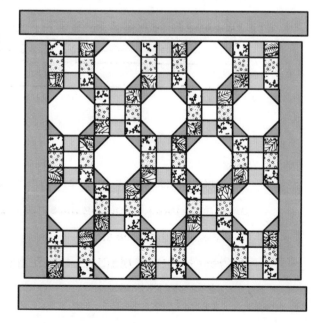

Finishing the Quilt

Planning Where to Quilt

The Basic Snowball Quilt

1. You may "stitch in the ditch" on the horizontal and vertical seams. Choose either invisible thread or a neutral color.

    OR

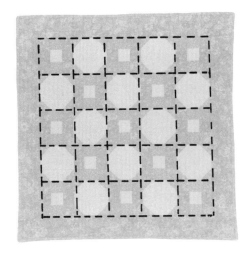

2. In the light snowball octagon and in the light center square of the Nine-Patch, you may stitch ¼" from the seam using matching thread.

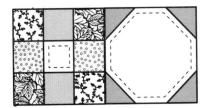

The Star Snowball Quilt

1. You may stitch diagonally along the center of the chains and outline stitch around the star. The diagonals can be stitched on either marked or unmarked lines. Lines can be marked with a long ruler and thin sliver of hard soap. Choose either invisible thread or thread to match the chains. If outlining the star, use a thread to match the snowball fabric and stitch ¼" from the seam.

    OR

2. You may "stitch in the ditch" on the horizontal and vertical seams. Choose either invisible thread or a neutral color.

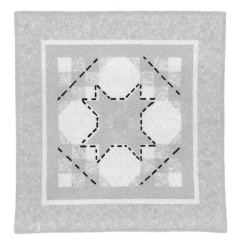

How much quilting and where to quilt depends on your level of skill and experience. You may choose to hand quilt the snowflake design after machine quilting the vertical and horizontal, or diagonal lines. However, hand quilting is not described in this book.

Marking the Optional Snowflake Design

For free motion machine quilting, it is recommended that a beginning quilter work on a Lap Size or smaller quilt. Only a more experienced machine quilter should free motion quilt a larger size.

If you have not yet marked the snowflake design as described on page 33, you may choose to trace the illustration on page 85 or to use a purchased stencil before layering and pinning the quilt.

Make certain that you can remove the marks from the fabric.

Preparing the Backing from 45" Wide Fabric

1. Following your Cutting Chart, fold the long backing crosswise and cut into equal pieces. If you custom fitted your quilt, you may need to adjust these measurements.

2. Remove the selvages and seam the backing pieces together.

Layering Quilt Top with Backing and Batting

1. Stretch out the backing right side down on a large floor area or table. Tape down on a floor area or clamp onto a table with large binder clips.

2. Place and smooth out the batting on top. Lay the quilt top right side up and centered on top of the batting. Completely smooth and stretch all layers until they are flat. Tape or clip securely. The backing and batting should extend at least 2" on all sides.

Safety Pin Basting

1. Place safety pins throughout the quilt away from the quilting path. If using optional snow-flake design, pin snowball block only through the four corner triangles.

2. Begin pinning in the center and work to the out-side, placing four pins in each block.

3. Grasp the opened pin in your right hand and the pinning tool in your left hand. Push the pin through the three layers, and bring the tip of the pin back out. Just as the tip of the pin surfaces, catch the tip in the grooved edge. To close, push pin down and click safety pin. If spoon pinning, twist the side of the spoon up while pushing down on the pin.

Machine Quilting

1. For straight line quilting, use a walking foot attachment which feeds the three layers evenly and prevents puckering. Choose either invisible thread or regular thread for the top of your machine. For the bobbin, use regular thread to match your backing material.

2. Lengthen your stitch to 8 - 10 stitches per inch, or a #3 setting.

3. Invisible thread only: Loosen the top tension.

4. Trim the backing and batting to within 2" of the outside edge of the quilt.

5. Roll the quilt tightly from the outside edge in toward middle.

6. Slide this roll into the keyhole of the sewing machine.

7. Place the needle in the depth of the seam and pull up the bobbin thread. Lock your threads with ½" of tiny stitches when you begin and end your sewing line. Run your hand underneath to feel for puckers.

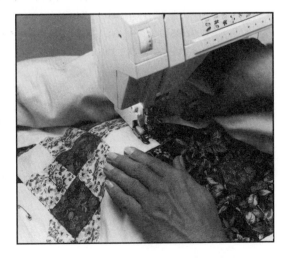

8. Place your hands flat on both sides of the needle. Keep the quilt area flat and tight. If you need to ease in the top fabric, feed the quilt through the machine by pushing the layers of fabric and bat-ting forward underneath the walking foot.

9. If puckering occurs, remove stitching by grasp-ing the bobbin thread with a pin or tweezers and pull gently to expose the invisible thread. Touch the invisible thread stitches with the rotary cutter blade as you pull the bobbin thread free from the quilt. Resew.

10. Unroll, roll, and machine quilt on all lines, sewing the length or width or diagonal of the quilt.

11. If outline stitching, use the edge of the walking foot as a guide. At corners, pivot with needle in.

Free Motion Quilting the Snowflake Design

This is a more advanced method of machine quilting using a darning foot attachment or a spring needle. You have the freedom to stitch forward, backward, and to the side without the use of a presser foot or feed dogs. However, this method requires practice.

Refer to your instruction manual for how to darn with your machine. You'll need to use a darning foot and drop or cover the feed dogs with a plate.

No stitch length is required as you control the length of the stitch. Lower the speed of your machine and use "needle down" position, if possible. Use a fine needle and a little hole throat plate if available. Use invisible thread or regular thread in the top, and thread to match your backing in the bobbin.

1. Before you begin to sew, study the diagram showing the direction for free motion quilting. This design is sewn in two stages. Working from the first starting point, follow the numbers to stitch every other loop. End stitching and begin at second starting point.

2. At the starting point, put the presser foot down. The quilt should move freely under the darning foot. Lower the needle and bring up the bobbin thread. Hold both threads. Move the fabric very slowly to lock the line with tiny stitches. Clip off the threads.

3. With your eyes watching the line ahead of the needle, and both hands grasping the fabric and acting as a quilting hoop, move the fabric in a steady motion while the machine is running at a constant speed. Do not move the fabric fast as this will result in large stitches and may even break the needle.

4. The size of the stitch is controlled by the speed of the movement. Keep the top of the block in the same position by moving the fabric from side to side and forward and backward.

5. When finishing a line, lock with tiny stitches and clip thread at the top. Tug bobbin thread slightly and cut.

Snowflake Stencil

Stage 1

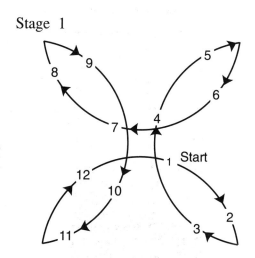

Stage 2

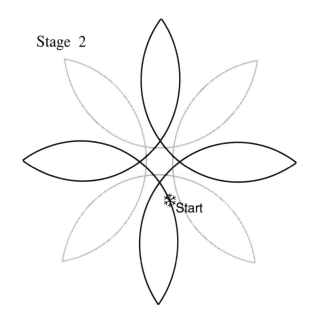

Adding the Binding

See page 79 for making a binding strip.

Use a walking foot attachment and regular thread on top and in the bobbin to match the backing. Use 10 stitches per inch, or #3 setting.

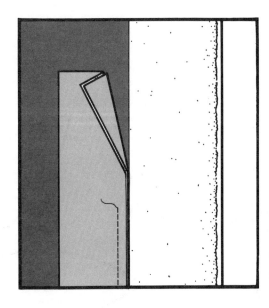

1. Line up the raw edges of the folded binding with the raw edge of the quilt top at the middle of one side.

2. Begin sewing 4" from the end of the binding.

3. At the corner, stop the stitching ¼" from the edge with the needle in the fabric. Raise the presser foot and turn the quilt to the next side. Put the foot back down.

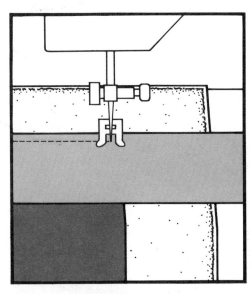

4. Sew backwards ¼" to the edge of the binding, raise the foot, and pull the quilt forward slightly.

5. Fold the binding strip straight up on the diagonal. Fingerpress in the diagonal fold.

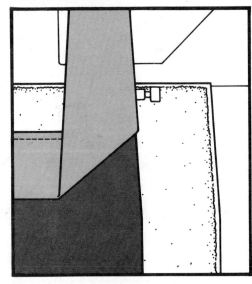

6. Fold the binding strip straight down with the diagonal fold underneath. Line up the top of the fold with the raw edge of the binding underneath.

7. Begin sewing from the corner.

8. Continue sewing and mitering the corners around the outside of the quilt.

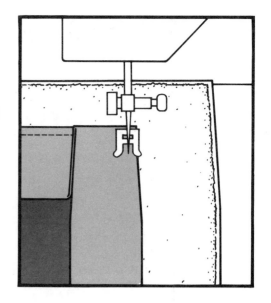

9. Stop sewing 4" from where the ends will overlap.

10. Line up the two ends of binding. Trim the excess with a ½" overlap. Open out the folded ends and pin right sides together. Sew a ¼" seam.

11. Continue to sew the binding in place.

12. Trim the batting and backing up to the raw edges of the binding.

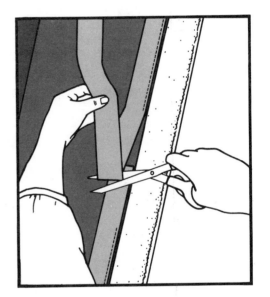

13. Fold the binding to the backside of the quilt. Pin in place so that the folded edge on the binding covers the stitching line. Tuck in the excess fabric at each miter on the diagonal.

14. On the back side of the quilt, finish by hand stitching in place.

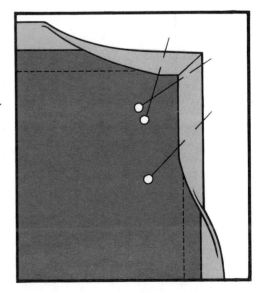

"Memories" Wallhanging

Approximate size 37" square

Nine Snowball Blocks with photo transfers, appliques, and embellishments.

A smaller four or six block wallhanging can be adapted from these instructions.

Position	Yardage	Cutting
Snowball	⅝ yd prewashed muslin, white or light fabric	(2) strips, 8 ½" x 45" into (9) 8 ½" squares
Lattice	⅜ yd dark, solid or appears solid	(4) strips, 2 ¾" x 45" into (24) 2 ¾" x 7" strips
Cornerstones	¼ yd medium to dark	(1) strip, 2 ¾" x 45" and (1) 2 ¾" square into (16) 2 ¾" squares
Snowball Corners	¼ yd medium	(2) strips, 2 ¼" x 45" into (36) 2 ¼" squares
First Border	¼ yd light or medium	(4) strips, 1 ½" x 45"
Second Border	⅝ yd medium to dark	(4) strips, 4 ½" x 45"
Binding	½ yd medium or dark	(4) strips, 3" x 45"
Backing	1 ⅜ yds light	
Lightweight Batting	42" x 42"	

Additional Supplies

Photographs, black and white or color, to be photocopied. The transfer process does not destroy the original photos.

Photo transfer medium such as Picture This™.

Embellishments (optional) such as lace, appliques, buttons, ribbons, beads, trinkets, or charms. A tacky glue to hold embellishments.

Fabric cut outs (optional) such as flowers, trees or animals. Cut around shape to include a ¼" seam allowance. Apply by applique.

7" square template plastic

Permanent fine marking pen (optional) for writing or touching-up photo transfers.

Making Photo Copies

Have the pictures photo copied in black and white or in color. Because the photo transfer process reverses the image and words, you may request to have the photo copy made in reverse or mirror image. Also, you may choose to have the image lightened because the image will take on the color of the background fabric.

It is recommended that you make one copy in mirror image and a second regular copy. Cut the regular copy into shapes for planning your layout. Cut up and use the mirror image for the actual photo transfer.

Arranging the Pieces

1. To visualize the finished blocks, cut the regular photo copies into shapes. Shapes can vary: square, rectangle, heart, circle or outline of figures.

2. Lay out the 8 ½" oversized Snowball Squares. Center and arrange the cut out photo copies with the optional embellishments to fit within a 6 ½" octagon. With the 7" square of template plastic make a "view-finder." Cut (2) 2 ¼" squares of your snowball corner fabric diagonally into four triangles. Glue onto the corners of the template. Plan each block as a unique fabric collage.

Transferring the Photo Copies onto Fabric

1. Transfer medium: Follow the instructions on your selected product. Most brands follow the same procedure. Generously apply the liquid gel to the right side of the photo copy cut out. According to your planned collage, place face down onto the 8 ½" square. The squares will be trimmed to 7" square after the 24 hour drying period.

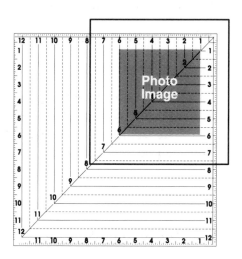

2. When thoroughly dried, moisten and rub off photo copy paper with corner of a sponge. After short drying period, rub off any remaining fuzz using a sponge. Rub in a circular motion. If outside edges are damaged, touch-up with permanent pen.

3. Using the view-finder, center the image. Mark dots at the four corners. Use the Square Up ruler to trim down to 7".

Making the Snowball Block

Add 2 ¼" square snowball corners according to Snowball Instructions starting on page 30. Do not touch iron to transfer image. It will melt and smear the image.

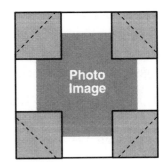

Applique Fabric Cut Outs (optional)

Cheater's Applique.

1. Cut out fabric shape with ¼" seam allowance.

2. Cut backing in same fabric.

3. Place right sides together. Using 20 stitches per inch or a small stitch, sew around the outline of the shape.

4. Trim seam allowance to ⅛". Cut an opening in the back and turn right side out. Finger press.

5. Blind-stitch applique onto the block by hand with matching thread.

Adding Optional Embellishments

Adding Lace to Photo Transfer

Choose a narrow flat lace.

Run a line of tacky glue along the outside edge of the photo transfer. Finger press lace into the wet glue. At corners, cut lace in diagonal miter. Cover corners with small bows, buttons or ribbon roses.

Adding Buttons, Trinkets and Charms

These embellishments can be sewn or glued on while the blocks are easily manageable. Delicate or heavy items can be added after the wallhanging is quilted.

Sewing the Wallhanging Together

1. Lay out blocks with lattice strips and cornerstones.

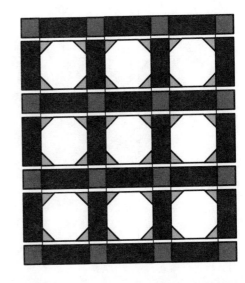

2. Working from left to right, assembly-line sew vertical rows together. Do not clip connecting threads. Carefully press seams away from Snowballs. To avoid touching the transfer, place seams along the edge of the ironing board.

3. Assembly-line sew horizontal seams. Push seams away from Snowball Blocks.

4. Add borders to the two sides. Press out and square off corners. Add the top and bottom borders. Press out and square off corners.

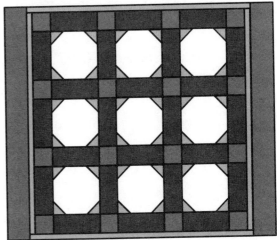

Finishing the Quilt

1. Cut 4" x 45" strip from the backing for a casing to hang the quilt. Set aside.

2. Layer and pin the quilt top, batting and backing according to the instructions on page 82.

3. Refer to machine quilting on page 83. Machine quilt by "stitching in the ditch" along the lattice and cornerstone seams. Stitch around the border seams.

4. Trim casing strip to 36" long. Hem the two short ends.

5. On the back of the quilt, draw a line 1 ½" above the top border seam. Center and place the casing below this line right sides together. Peel back the quilt top and batting. Sew through only the casing and backing ¼" down from the line.

6. Flip casing strip up and pin through the quilt backing, batting and quilt top.

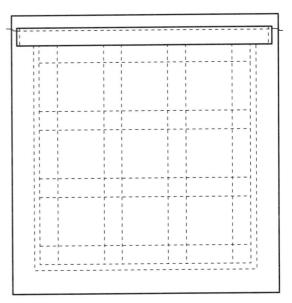

Stained Glass Swag

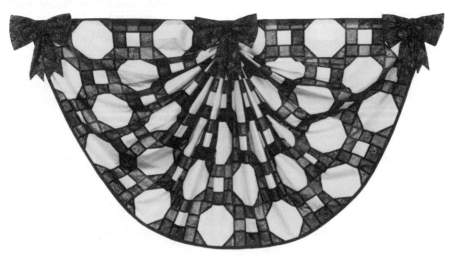

Approximate size 33" x 104".   Fits window up to 68" wide.

The swag hangs about 33" in length. Add or subtract blocks to custom fit your window.
The stained glass effect is most dramatic when using jewel tone colors in the quilt. As an
option, the swag can be backed with white fabric to prevent the sun from fading colors.

Materials

Refer to Twin size Basic Snowball Quilt yardage on page 16. Purchase fabric as listed for
Nine-Patch and Snowball Blocks. Do not purchase border and other fabrics.

For a Scrap option, cut (27) 2 ¾" x 45" random strips for making Nine-patch blocks. Make
three sets each: Sections A, B and C.

Supplies

3 yds	Backing (optional)	
⅝ yd	Binding (optional)	cut (5) 3" x 45" strips
¾ yd	Bows	cut (3) 11" x 12" pieces (3) 6" x 20" strips
	Lightweight Batting for Bows	cut (3) 6" x 11" pieces

Large safety pins for holding fan fold

Curtain rod to fit your window. It may be a single plain rod, or double rod for hanging sheer
or curtain behind swag.

Wire or twist tie to hang swag on rod.

Making the Swag

1. Follow the Twin size Basic Snowball instructions starting on page 19 to make 40 Nine-Patch and 40 Snowball Blocks.

2. When sewing the blocks together, make 32 paired blocks. See page 34.

3. Make 16 Sets of Four.

4. When sewing the sets together, lay out rows with 8 sets down and 2 sets across.

5. With the remaining 16 blocks, follow instructions for the right side row.

6. The finished swag will have 5 rows across and 16 rows down.

7. Optional backing, a quick turn with no binding:

   Center swag right sides together on backing. Pin and sew along two short sides and one long side, leaving top open. Trim backing and clip corners. Turn right side out and press. If you choose, pin baste and machine quilt along outlines of blocks. Machine baste ¼" from top raw edges. Skip to Fan Folding Top Edge of Swag.

   OR

8. Binding with no backing:

   Follow the binding instructions starting on page 86 to sew binding on two short sides and one long side. The remaining long side will be fan folded and concealed with a bow.

   OR

9. Binding with backing:

   Lay down backing with the wrong side up. Center swag right side up. Pin along two short sides and one long side. Trim backing to size of swag. Follow the binding instructions starting on page 86 to sew binding on pinned sides. If you choose, pin baste and machine quilt along outlines of blocks. Machine baste ¼" from top raw edges.

Fan Folding Top Edge of Swag

Working along the top edge, start at one end and fold block in half, right side out. Continue fan folding the length of the top edge. With a large safety pin, pin through the center of the top folded edge. If one pin is insufficient, use two pins or sew through all thicknesses by hand.

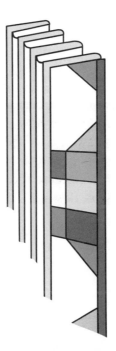

Making Three Bows

With right sides together fold 11" x 12" pieces in half, making them 11" x 6". Pin batting in place underneath. Sew along three raw edges leaving 3" opening in the middle of the long side. Clip corners and turn right side out. Finger press or stitch across opening.

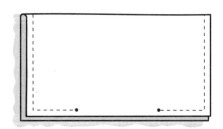

Making Three Bow Ties

With right sides together fold the 6" x 20" strips in half, making them 3" x 20". At each end mark a dot ¼" in from the corners. Using the point of a ruler, draw a "V" connecting the dot with the folded edge. Sew along the raw edges and "V" at each end, leaving a 3" opening in the middle of the long side. Trim "V" points and turn right side out. Finger press or stitch across opening.

Assembling the Bows

Hand pleat the center of the bow. Fold the center of the Tie, making it 1" wide. Wrap the Tie around the center of the Bow. Machine or hand stitch Tie in place.

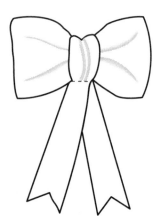

Hanging the Swag

Wrap a wire or twist tie around the large safety pin and connect it to the center of the curtain rod. Pin or sew the Bow in place to cover the top raw edge of the swag. At the two remaining corners, place a safety pin and connect to rod with wire. Conceal with Bows.

Index

Order Information

If you do not have a quilt shop in your area, you may write for a complete catalog and current price list of all books and patterns published by Quilt in a Day®, Inc.

Books

Quilt in a Day Log Cabin
The Sampler—A Machine Sewn Quilt
Trio of Treasured Quilts
Lover's Knot Quilt
Amish Quilt in a Day
Irish Chain in a Day
Country Christmas
May Basket Quilt
Diamond Log Cabin Tablecloth or Treeskirt
Morning Star Quilt
Trip Around the World Quilt
Dresden Plate Quilt, A Simplified Method
Pineapple Quilt, a Piece of Cake
Radiant Star Quilt
Blazing Star Tablecloth
Tulip Quilt
Scrap Quilt, Strips and Spider Webs
Burgoyne Surrounded
Sunbonnet Sue Visits Quilt in a Day
Creating With Color
Christmas Quilts and Crafts
Quilter's Year
Baskets & Flowers
Quilters Almanac
Christmas Traditions
Stars Across America
Kaleidoscope
Machine Quilting Primer
Jewel Box Quilt
Nana's Garden

Booklets and Patterns

Patchwork Santa
Last Minute Gifts
Angel of Antiquity
Log Cabin Wreath Wallhanging
Log Cabin Christmas Tree Wallhanging
Flying Geese Quilt
Miniature May Basket Wallhanging
Tulip Table Runner and Wallhanging
Heart's Delight, Nine-Patch Variations
Country Flag Wallhanging
Spools and Tools Wallhanging
Schoolhouse Wallhanging
Star for all Seasons

Videos

Log Cabin Video
Lover's Knot Video
Irish Chain Video
Ohio Star Video
Blazing Star Video
Scrap Quilt Video
Morning Star Video
Trip Around the World Video
Pineapple Video
Radiant Star Video
Flying Geese Video
and many others

If you are ever in San Diego County, southern California, drop by the Quilt in a Day center quilt shop a classroom in the La Costa Meadows Industrial Park. Write ahead for a current class schedule and map. Eleanor Burns may be seen on Public Broadcasting Stations (PBS) throughout the country. Check TV listings in your area.

Quilt in a Day, Inc.
1955 Diamond Street, San Marcos, California 92069-5122
www.quiltinaday.com • e-mail: qiad@quiltinaday.com
Orders: 800 777-4852 fax: 760 591-4424